D0269565

The Magic of Well-Being

The Magic _of_ Well-Being

JUDITH JACKSON

DORLING KINDERSLEY
London • New York • Stuttgart • Moscow

656101

MORAY COUNCIL
DEPARTMENT OF TECHNICAL
& LEISURE SERVICES
613

A DORLING KINDERSLEY BOOK

This book celebrates the life of my aunt, Edith Allen. Her
beauty, strength, and spirit inspired my pursuit
of the life-expanding information within
these pages. I am forever in her debt.

IMPORTANT NOTICE
This is not a medical reference book. The information it
contains is general, not specific to any individual or
group. The opinions expressed are those of the
author and reflect her personal philosophy.

PROJECT EDITOR	Susie Behar
PROJECT ART EDITOR	Deborah Myatt
SENIOR MANAGING EDITOR	Mary-Clare Jerram
MANAGING ART EDITOR	Amanda Lunn
PRODUCTION	Alison Jones
PHOTOGRAPHER	Andy Crawford

First published in Great Britain in 1997 by
Dorling Kindersley Limited 9 Henrietta Street,
London WC2 8PS

Copyright © 1997 Dorling Kindersley Limited, London
Text copyright © 1997 Judith Jackson

Visit us on the World Wide Web at http://www.dk.com

All rights reserved. No part of this publication may be
reproduced, stored in a retrieval system, or transmitted
in any form or by any means, electronic, mechanical,
photocopying, recording, or otherwise, without the
prior written permission of the copyright owners.

A CIP catalogue record for this book is available
from the British Library

ISBN 0-7513-0262-7

Computer page make-up by Mark Bracey and
Deborah Myatt, Dorling Kindersley, Great Britain
Text film output by The Right Type, Great Britain
Reproduced by Colourpath, Great Britain
Printed and bound by Star Standard, Singapore

CONTENTS

SENSORY SAFARI

LET'S TAKE A JOURNEY. It could be the most exciting, challenging, and rewarding one of your whole life. The destination is the magical kingdom of well-being. You are going to arrive there by utilizing your most powerful built-in vehicle — your senses. Hold on, because you can ride far and wide on the wings of your five senses — touch, taste, smell, hearing, and sight. And you can soar inwards on your

CALM CONTROL

sixth "knowing sense", or intuition. *The Magic of Well-Being* describes a variety of tried-and-tested techniques that will transform the way you look, feel, and cope with every-day challenges. If you are troubled by tension, fatigue, and depression, I have devised simple and fun activities that overcome these common blocks to total well-being.

SOOTHING FRAGRANCE

When I first studied, and then began a professional practice in the art and science of aromatherapy I soon realized that nature intends us to use all our senses to live in blissful balance. This has been my mission in my practice and teaching, and now with this book. Well-being should be more than just staying alive; it should be living more fully in every

AROMATHERAPY MASSAGE

moment, while looking and feeling great. The extent to which you are "sensory aware" is a measure of your capacity for life. How you use your senses will help you tune into what is good for you in terms of what you eat and drink, how you exercise, how long you sleep, and much else. Sensory awareness is your natural genetic heritage, and a gift to be cherished.

JUDITH JACKSON

HOW TO USE THIS BOOK

You can be your own stress therapist, personal trainer, aromatherapist, and nutritionist if you follow this unique programme, step by sensory step.

THIS BOOK IS DIVIDED into two sections. The first part provides you with the basic skills required for the second part. Learning part one's techniques – Calm Control, Relaxion (an original exercise routine), Aromatherapy, and Sensory Food – is the key to realizing the full benefit of the Rescue Routines in part two. These routines are 24-hour programmes that take you activity by activity through a whole day and night of relief and restoration. Whatever your immediate mental, physical, or lifestyle worry, you should be able to find relevant advice. You will no longer panic if you wake up feeling fat or frantic; pick up *The Magic of Well-Being* and discover the Rescue you need.

Use the techniques and Rescue Routines to help you to be what nature intends you to be: a balanced human being, fully aware in the present. When you are in this optimum state, in blissful union with nature and responsive to your Knowing Sense, you will experience how magical it is to be truly well.

TEST YOUR SENSES

Answer these questions with Always (10 points), Sometimes (5 points), or Never (no points), and discover how in touch you are with your senses.

1. Are you turned on by certain smells, such as flowers or perfume?

2. Do you enjoy giving a massage to someone you don't know?

3. Do you enjoy the feel of certain textures, such as silk or animal fur?

4. Are you transported by certain sounds, such as music?

5. Does eating really delicious food render you ecstatic?

6. Do you enjoy receiving a massage from someone you don't know?

7. Are you reminded of places and people when you detect certain odours?

8. Do you look after your eyes, taking care to rest them occasionally?

9. If you are short-sighted or long-sighted, do you wear glasses regularly?

10. Do you listen carefully to what is being said, or to music, or to other sounds?

11. Do you eat slowly and take the time to taste your food properly?

12. Do you give your eyes a feast once in a while, with art, for instance?

TOTAL SCORE

These questions should make you think about how you use and how in touch you are with your senses; your total score will give you an indication of your level of sensory awareness.

Everyone can score the maximum 120 points, since the questions relate to basic sensory awareness. If your score is 80 or under, you are probably neglecting an important area of your life.

THE SLANT BOARD

Use this board for physical and mental relaxation. Lying with your head lower than your feet rests the internal organs and feeds the brain with blood. Inversion reverses the negative effects of gravity and promotes rejuvenation.

The board should measure 2 m (6 ft) long and 60 cm (2 ft) wide. Make one with a sturdy piece of plywood, elevated 35 cm (14 in) at one end. It may help to prevent sliding if you attach a strap to the foot end.

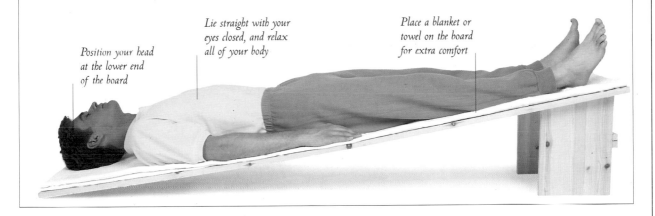

Position your head at the lower end of the board

Lie straight with your eyes closed, and relax all of your body

Place a blanket or towel on the board for extra comfort

RESCUE GUIDELINES

Each Rescue Routine suggests a special programme for the day. Below are some of the themes that run through all of them.

COLOURS & CLOCKS ▶
Each Rescue Routine suggests colours to wear on that day to enhance its theme. Times for activities are also given, but these are only guidelines.

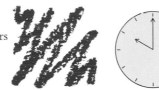

◀ HOT WATER & LEMON
Replace your regular morning caffeinated drink with hot water. Cleansing and refreshing, it cuts through the cobwebs of the night.

CONTACT WITH NATURE ▶
Each Rescue suggests ways in which unity with nature can put us in touch with ourselves as we breathe, walk, and connect with earth, rock, and tree.

NUDGE NOTES

Come up with phrases to help you make the most of a particular Rescue Routine. Jot them down and put them where you can't miss the message. Alternatively, write out the Nudge Notes I have suggested for each Rescue. Use these little notes as reminders to spark positive thought and action. They are inspiring self-talk that is tangible, helpful, and even entertaining.

"Clean inside, gorgeous outside"

"Breathe!"

"Slant rest is best"

"This is my day"

ASSESS YOUR WELL-BEING

This test enables you to do a little self-diagnosis, though an in-depth assessment of your health would have to come from a doctor. However, if you reply to these questions honestly, the answers should give you an idea of your strengths and weaknesses, and which of my Rescue Routines you most need. Write your score in the coloured square beside each question. Add up the points for each colour and then refer to the scoring section opposite to assess your well-being.

ALWAYS : 15 • SOMETIMES : 10 • RARELY : 5 • NEVER : 0

1. Do you feel guilty if you make time for pleasure?

2. Do you wonder if life is really worth the effort?

3. Do you think that you are "naturally" overweight?

4. Is it hard to sit down and relax for more than ten minutes at a time?

5. Are you concerned about growing older?

6. Do you have a feeling of impending disaster?

7. When you eat something naughty, like a rich chocolate cake, are you unable to fully enjoy it?

8. Do you need to take laxatives to facilitate an easy bowel movement every day?

9. Do you use caffeine to give you a quick energy lift?

10. Does the thought of living many years scare you?

11. Do you regularly feel tired and lacking in energy?

12. Do you eat many refined foods, such as white bread and sugar?

13. Are you one of the first people to finish your meal?

14. Do you find it difficult not to interrupt another's conversation?

15. Do you take your work worries with you into your private life?

16. Do you delay dieting for a "better" time, such as after your holiday?

17. When you travel on business, are you too busy to enjoy any new culture around you?

18. When you wake up in the morning, do you dread facing the day ahead?

19. Do you equate old age with disability?

20. Do you have frequent tension headaches?

21. Does your temper have a shorter fuse than it used to?

22. When you walk up a flight of stairs are you short of breath?

23. Do you see the down side to everything? Is your glass half empty as opposed to half full?

24. Do you eat when you aren't hungry, just because it's time?

25. Do you think you are unworthy of a treat?

26. Are you always finding excuses not to exercise in fresh air?

27. Do you have trouble going to sleep because you are too keyed up or find yourself worrying?

28. Does a wrinkle or two cause you distress?

29. Do you drink less than six glasses of pure water daily?

30. Do you only socialize with people your own age?

31. Do you find it difficult to start your day without coffee, tea, or other stimulants?

32. Do you need, not just desire, alcohol to unwind after work?

33. Do you have a low self-image because of your weight?

34. Have you lost your desire to spend time with other people?

35. Do you find yourself no longer pursuing sports or hobbies because you are too tired?

36. Are you unaware of pesticides and preservatives in your food?

WELL-BEING SCORE

To evaluate your state of well-being, add together the scores for each colour and enter the total in the appropriate box. Identify the relevant Rescues.

Depression

0–25: you are quite optimistic • 26–50: you may have a tendency towards depression • 51–75: you should act on my anti-depression suggestions. See pages 82–85

Toxicity

0–25: your lifestyle is basically healthy • 26–50: try to be more health-aware • 51–75: you should pay much more attention to exercise and diet. See pages 66–69

Stress

0–30: you have a stress-free lifestyle • 31–60: you could think about lowering your stress level • 61–90: you need my stress-relief day. See pages 62–65, 86–89

Diet and Weight Control

0–25: your attitude to eating is balanced and healthy • 26–50: you may have some unhealthy eating habits • 51–75: follow my dietary suggestions. See pages 48–51, 70–73

Fatigue

0–25: you are full of energy • 26–50: you could improve your energy level • 51–75: you need to raise your energy level with my Rescue. See pages 74–77

Self-indulgence

0–25: you are living well • 26–50: you could think about getting more out of life • 51–75: give yourself full permission to enjoy your life. See pages 90–93

Age

0–25: whatever your years, you are young • 26–50: age is beginning to bother you • 51–75: try my anti-ageing Rescue and feel young again. See pages 78–81

THE KEYS TO WELL-BEING

The first part of this book sets you on the path to well-being with self-development techniques, used again in the Rescue Routines. My unique yet simple Calm Control, Relaxion, Aromatherapy, and Sensory Food practices are designed to meet challenges to mind, body, and spirit. The magic key that unlocks the door to the life you have always hoped for is sensory awareness. Be totally present in the following activities and you will multiply their benefits tenfold. You will soon arrive at your desired destination — optimum well-being.

CALM CONTROL

THE BASIS of all the activities in this book is Calm Control. If you are in a state of Calm Control, you act rather than react. You control a situation and its effect on you, rather than the other way around. You receive more from anything positive you do for yourself, whether eating, exercising, bathing, massaging, or just resting. Most importantly, you will radically reduce the amount of stress in your life. This chapter takes you into four powerful methods that can help you access that control: Meditation, Contemplation, Visualization, and Transformations. When you centre yourself in one of these techniques, you feel unified within yourself and with your surroundings. For instance, if you are pressing your spine against a tree, and totally concentrate on the experience, you become the tree. This truly expands the experience to a more exhilarating level. The great thing is that this transforming awareness can be with you wherever you are, in any situation. When you call upon it, you will be in Calm Control. Taking up the techniques of Calm Control as a way of life will give you the opportunity to live more fully and with more joy.

TRANQUIL VISTAS

PEACEFUL SKIES

NATURE'S BEAUTY

MANDALA MEDITATION

My system of meditation puts you in touch with your six senses, including your knowing sense (or intuition), giving you a new awareness of yourself.

MEDITATION OFFERS a unique opportunity for going deep within yourself to find out what you really have in there. It should be a mental cleansing to clear the mind of the cacophony of thoughts that criss-cross its neural pathways every waking hour. Meditating regularly will help you to feel in command of yourself, focused, and more objective.

My system of meditation, Mandala Meditation, combines the sensory awareness of Tantric yoga with the relaxation of Transcendental Meditation. It is designed to connect you in a circle of existence with the universe, linking every thought, desire, and feeling with nature, and the whole, complete you. It will put you in touch with yourself.

Mandala Meditation is portable. All you need is somewhere to sit quietly for 20 minutes. You can begin by repeating a mantra (a symbolic word or phrase) to guide you into the right mood. It can be difficult to find the concentration required for meditation. You may, for instance, be unable to stop distracting thoughts from popping into your mind. If this happens, gently push the thought aside, making a brief mental note to consider it after meditating. You could choose to contemplate the thought at a later time *(see p.18)*.

Quiet is essential for meditation. Take the phone off the hook, and tell family members not to disturb you. In your home, designate a quiet area as your meditation space.

HOW TO SIT

Your sitting posture affects the quality of your meditation. Comfort is key.

Since you will be sitting still for 20 minutes, you need to be comfortable. Sitting with a straight back enhances the calming effects of meditation, since the nerves most critical to your overall well-being run up the spine. Sitting cross-legged, which keeps the body balanced and spine straight, is the best pose. If your knees and hips are not flexible enough, support yourself with pillows, or sit on a straight-backed chair. Close your eyes and rest your hands on your knees.

Relax your body

Wear loose comfortable clothes

THE MANDALA

Symbolic pictures with spiritual messages, known as mandalas, have instructed and inspired for thousands of years. The Sanskrit word "mandala" is taken from sacred Indian texts and means circle. The circle represented the cosmos, or total universe. Psychiatrist Carl Jung used mandalas as a unifying representation of self. Mandala meditation brings you full circle into balance.

HOW TO MEDITATE

Sit comfortably, wearing a shawl or blanket to keep you warm. Scent the room with a calming essence, and play soft music. As you move through the first half of the meditation, you will be creating a sensory environment for the ultimate experience.

1 INHALE THE SCENT

Close your eyes and deeply breathe the scented air. As the odour neurons lining your nasal passages transmit the fragrance deep within your brain, feel its message in your entire being. Be scent-aware for two minutes.

2 ABSORB THE MUSIC

Listen to the music. Imagine the receptors in your ears registering every note. Tune into and identify each instrument and its unique sound. Do you hear violins or cellos? Breathe deeply as you analyze the music. Concentrate wholly on the music for two minutes.

3 EXPLORE TASTE

Now awaken your sense of taste. Every taste — sweet, sour, salty, bitter, pungent, or astringent — has its own territory on the tongue. Bathe your tongue in digestive juices stored in the mouth. Let the tip register imagined sweetness, the back bitterness, the sides sourness, the surface saltiness. Savour these imagined tastes for two minutes.

CALMING FRAGRANCES
Let airborne fragrances, such as calming lavender, vetiver, or clary sage, lead you into meditation.

4 EXPERIENCE TOUCH

We need to touch our world in order to relate to it, to touch our bodies to know that we are functioning. With your fingertips, gently stroke the fabric of your clothing. Is it smooth, rough, warm, or cool? Is the texture interesting? Feel your body's contact with the chair or mat on which you are sitting. Fully experience these tactile sensations for two minutes.

5 LOOK INWARD

The eye is your camera on the world. But to go deeply into the sight sense, your eyes must be closed. Imagine that you are breathing light into your eyes. The light forms an image in your "mind's eye." Choose an image that brings you a sense of deep peace. See, for instance, a green hill covered with brightly coloured flowers, or a clear blue sky. Focus on your chosen scene for two minutes.

6 KNOWING

The deepest experience will come when you tune into your knowing sense (or intuition). This sense talks to the conscious and subconscious you, and communicates with every cell in your body. For ten minutes, turn your attention inwards to that peaceful place where conscious thoughts cease. If a worldly thought intrudes, focus on your breathing.

CONTEMPLATION

Contemplation as a creative thought form has been sacrificed to modern world distractions. Return a few contemplative moments to every day's schedule and you will venture into new self-territory.

CONTEMPLATION is the ancient art of considered thought — something that our modern world is not attuned to. When you contemplate, you examine and develop an idea with no censure or distraction. You consciously work with focused thought, delving deeply into every meaning. You may well find that this process gives you the creative brain space in which to answer important questions, discover new ideas, and form considered, thoughtful, and unbiased opinions. It is best to contemplate alone. Although you can contemplate in an area full of people, it is very difficult without a lot of practice. One way to hone your thought processes is to begin by reading inspiring philosophical essays and poetry. It may help to have a special place solely for contemplation, an idea long accepted in Asia. If you are unable to physically retreat to your "thinking house", create a special space in your mind.

THE FOUR STEPS

The many distractions of our "getting" and "spending" world make it necessary to consciously plan contemplation.

1 To begin, find a quiet place where you can be alone, serene, comfortable, and able to just think. Consider this place your own "thinking house" to which you can retreat when you need to really think. Nature provides the most nurturing space in which to contemplate. If weather or location dictate indoor contemplation, surround yourself with as much greenery as possible, and put a closed door between you and distracting movement and noise.

2 Relax, take off your shoes, and take several deep breaths. If you are very tense, spend several minutes releasing your muscles, starting at the feet and working upwards. You may want to scent the air with essence of lavender or sandalwood.

3 Select a thought that deserves your concentration and give it your full attention. If the subject is familiar, try to mentally challenge yourself with a fresh point of view.

4 Sweep intruding thoughts out of your mind. This is a rare opportunity to thoroughly explore a single subject. We live in a world of idea surfing, never diving deep enough, and so depriving ourselves and our relationships of true understanding. Spend at least 30 minutes in your thinking house.

MAGICAL NATURE

Contemplate in an area of natural beauty, where you can feel peaceful. Hug a tree. Concentrate on this magnificent example of how nature gives and receives in a life-sustaining balance. As psychologist and author Thomas Moore says "... the answer to the riddle of life is often found in the forest, the place where trees congregate and cast their spell."

VISUALIZATION

Enhance a positive experience as well as dispel the harmful effects of a negative one with visualization. Put on your rose-coloured glasses and fill your fields with flowers instead of weeds. It's the only way to grow.

PROJECTING POSITIVE images onto your mind's inner screen can help keep you well and happy. Known as visualization, it is an important companion to meditation and contemplation. Scientific studies have shown that powerfully focused visualization can lead to faster rates of healing for broken bones. If your leg is broken and you want to visualize the bone mending, ask for a copy of the X-ray. Visualize it mending several times during the day and before you go to sleep at night.

A new view can mean a new you. Feeling overweight? Visualize what you will look like in the near future when you have reached a healthy weight. You will look better even before you lose the weight and your more slender image becomes a reality. You will pull in your stomach and stand taller to meet your expectation. When you are not feeling well, it is easy to slip into negativity and think depressing thoughts. The more negativity, the more likely you are to be ill. Instead, visualize yourself well and enjoying every minute of your newfound vitality in your favourite holiday spot. You will surely be there sooner.

At work if you are facing a tough meeting or just need a break, a few minutes of positive visualization can lift your spirits and improve your confidence. Make yourself comfortable and visualize a rewarding scene.

THE FIVE STEPS

You must start with a clean mental canvas, project a definite image, and hold the vision long enough to be effective.

1 First, relax your body. Mentally breathe into each area, starting at the feet, and then release that part on your exhalation.

2 Push aside thoughts unrelated to the visualization. The stronger your "picture", the easier this is.

3 Give the desired action a setting. For instance, if you want to imagine being given a salary raise, put the scene in your boss's office.

4 Bring all your senses into play. The more real you make your visualization, the more powerful will be its benefits. See the location in all its details, including colour scheme, furnishings, paintings on the wall. How would it smell? What would the temperature be?

5 The length of your visualization time is not as important as the quality of concentration. If you are totally "in" it, five minutes will work.

WELL-BEING FOCUS

If you are feeling ill, visualize yourself running, dancing, and singing at the edge of the waves. Smell the salt air, and feel the cool water rush between your toes. Focus on a fun activity, such as wind-surfing or flying a kite. Congratulate yourself on making such a speedy recovery.

TRANSFORMATIONS

By practising these simple transformation techniques, you can learn how to use time rather than let it abuse you.

FINDING JOY in life's occasionally frustrating circumstances is a challenge to mind, body, and spirit. Even small frustrations, such as a seemingly endless red traffic light, can trigger the release of hormones that reduce the immune system's response and damage the heart by contracting arteries; the release is caused by our reaction to an event, not the event itself.

If you learn to think of delays and various road-blocks to progress as unexpected gifts of time and rare opportunities, you can transform them by turning negatives into positives. To quote doctor and author Deepak Chopra, "by becoming self-aware you gain ownership of reality. In becoming real, you become master of inner and outer life."

For example, if you are held up in traffic, instead of becoming stressed, improve muscle tone and relieve tension by performing a few simple exercises. When sitting at your desk, mentally blocked, try my seated exercises and see the difference to mind and body. These transformation techniques may become your most useful coping alchemy.

HAND EXERCISES

If you are stuck in a traffic jam in your car, use these steering wheel exercises to relieve frustration and improve hand flexibility.

◀ To strengthen your wrists, grip the top of the steering wheel firmly. Then roll your hands forward and back about ten times.

▶ This exercise strengthens your fingers and increases their flexibility. Place your fingertips on the wheel. Push hard, forcing the fingers to bend, then relax. Repeat six times.

◀ Playing the steering wheel like a piano with your fingertips will increase their flexibility. Play on the rim for about two minutes.

MOBILE EDUCATION

Prepare for any situation where you might have to wait by having a book on hand. Make a habit of reading material that educates and inspires.

TENSION RELIEVER

In a tense situation, in the office or in your car, relieve stress by squeezing a tennis or rubber ball. Hold it in your hand, squeeze hard, and release several times.

SITTING EXERCISES

These exercises will ease muscular tension and loosen joints wherever you are sitting, be it at your work desk, or even buckled into a plane seat.

HEAD & NECK

If you have been seated for a while, this exercise can stimulate the blood flow and make you feel brighter. Clasp your hands behind your head, elbows back. Push your head against your hands as hard as you can. Hold for a count of ten.

Clasp your hands at the base of your skull

Push your head against your hands

SHOULDERS & BACK

The spine needs a good stretch once in a while to keep it flexible. Do this exercise at your desk or while waiting. Grasp the back of the chair seat with the right hand. Place your left arm across your body and hold the right side of the seat. Turn your head to look over your left shoulder. Hold for ten seconds. Repeat on the other side.

Your legs should face forwards with your feet flat on the ground

HAMSTRINGS, HIPS, & BACK

This stretch relieves tension in the hamstrings and neck. Wrap your arms and hands around one leg just below the knee. Pull the knee to your forehead. Hold for ten counts. Repeat three times on each leg.

Bring your head to your knee and feel the back of your neck stretch

Pull the leg inwards and upwards as far as you can

RELAXION

DAWN ENERGY

AWAKEN THE NATURAL ability of the body to unwind, tone, and shape itself with my simple easy-to-learn exercise routine, Relaxion. This combines movement, breathing, visualization (see p.20), and sensory awareness. Relaxion's many benefits range from lower blood pressure and increased suppleness to a calmer, clearer, and more positive mind. As you perform the exercises, concentrate

FRAGRANT AIR

on each movement by putting your mind in your muscles and listening to your body. Transform exercising into a pleasurable, sensuous experience. Accompany the movements with soothing rhythmic instrumental music, and fill your exercise room with sensuous scents and fresh flowers. The full exercise programme takes about 30 minutes, but you can perform a shorter version, working from the first exercise up to the Lying Leg and Hip Stretch (see p.27) in 15 minutes. Although my stretching exercises are suitable for most people, if you are in any doubt, check with your doctor before you begin the exercise programme. Never push yourself to do something that is painful. Find a time slot that suits you, then stick to it. Make exercising part of your daily routine and you will soon experience the remarkable benefits to your mind, body, and spirit.

PLEASING ENVIRONMENT

RELAXION ROUTINE

*Before you begin my exercises, here are some basic techniques
to help you practise safely and achieve maximum benefit.*

CORRECT BREATHING is a key element to exercising well. Breathing deeply from the diaphragm assists movement and relaxation. The general rule is to breathe in on muscle contraction, and out on relaxation. Between each movement, take long, deep breaths, breathing in through the nose and out through the mouth. Protecting your back is also very important. Push your lower back into the floor during all of the movements that require you to lie on your back. Push your pelvis into the floor when lying on your stomach. Perform each exercise rhythmically. Although I have suggested how many times you should perform each exercise, never force yourself to the point of exhaustion.

RELAXED POSE

Begin the Relaxion routine by lying on the floor in the relaxed pose. This exercise releases the mind and body in preparation for the exercises. Lie flat on your back with your arms at your sides, palms up. Bend your knees but keep your back and feet flat on the floor. Take four deep breaths. Feel your stomach and diaphragm expand as you inhale. Relax and breathe out normally.

WHAT TO WEAR

Wear comfortable cotton clothes that allow your skin to breathe. Do not wear anything constricting. Exercise in bare feet and use a rug or yoga mat to prevent slipping. It is important to feel warm, so if the room is cold, wear a tracksuit.

WARM~UP MOVEMENTS

*These exercises prepare the body for more challenging stretches
to follow. Always stretch only as far as is comfortable.*

▶ Lie with your arms over your head. Stretch the right arm and leg, the left arm and leg, then both arms and legs together.

Stretch your leg as far as possible

Press the straight leg into the floor

▲ Lie on your back. Clasp one knee and pull it towards your chest. Keep your back straight.

Push your lower back into the floor

▲ Straighten your leg as far as possible, keeping your hands flat on the floor. Lower your leg.

Keep your leg as straight as possible

◀ Bend your knee and bring your head up to meet it. Repeat the routine on the other side.

THE EXERCISES

Move from one exercise to the next as fluidly as possible.
Remember to relax and breathe after each exercise.

FOETAL POSITION STRETCH

As you stretch, visualize yourself as comfortable and relaxed as possible. It should be easy, since you will end up in the foetal position, the position of the foetus within the mother's womb and our most basic pose.
• **BENEFITS** Releases the lower back muscles and stretches the vertebrae and thighs.

Make sure your back is flat on the floor

"My whole being is safe and relaxed"

1 Lie on your back with your arms by your sides and the palms of your hands flat on the floor. Bend your knees.

Raise your head as far as possible

2 Raise both knees and pull them towards your chest. Raise your head and try to touch your knees with your forehead. Do not strain.

As you roll, let your arms and shoulders roll with you

3 Lower your head and return your feet to the floor, keeping your knees bent. Roll your whole body gently over onto one side. Roll onto your back and over to the other side, before returning to the centre.

LOWER BACK STRETCH

Visualize stretching the lower back, and as you do this, imagine each vertebra settling into its correct place along the length of the spine.
• **BENEFITS** Tightens and trims the waist. Also frees and strengthens the lower back.

"I'm loosening my entire spinal column"

1 Lie on your back with your legs in a half-raised position and your feet flat on the floor. Stretch out your arms so that they are parallel to your shoulders.

2 Drop your knees all the way to the floor, twisting your hips with your legs. Return to the starting position. Repeat on the same side 12 times. Begin again on the other side.

LYING LEG & HIP STRETCH

Visualize your leg reaching for the ceiling with all your energy flowing upwards.
• **BENEFITS** Stretches the hamstrings (the large tendons in the back of the legs), calves, and ankles.

Straighten your leg as far as possible

Lie on the floor with your arms at your sides, palms down. Raise your left leg, keeping your right leg on the floor. When the left leg is fully extended flex the foot, then straighten and lower the leg. Repeat with the right leg. Perform three times with each leg.

Keep your foot on the floor, toes pointed

Your head should remain on the floor

TUMMY TONE

Visualize your stomach muscles (they run vertically and horizontally) working hard, and your pelvis supporting your stomach.
• **BENEFITS** Tones the stomach area.

Keep your knees bent throughout the stretch

1 Lie on your back. Bend your knees, keeping your feet on the floor. Place your hands beneath your head.

2 Raise your head and chest towards your knees, tilting your pelvis upwards and contracting your stomach muscles. Return your head to the floor. Repeat 20 times.

TORSO & BACK STRETCH

Visualize the torso twisting forward. Concentrate on your stomach muscles.
• **BENEFITS** Trims the waist, stretches the back, and tightens the stomach muscles.

"My stomach muscles are working"

With your knees half-bent, your feet on the floor, and your hands behind your head, raise your head and chest and touch your left knee with your right elbow. Repeat 20 times, alternating sides.

Try to keep your foot on the floor as you stretch

SPINE ROCK

Imagine that you are holding your body in the foetal position. This will help you to rock back and forth smoothly. Feel the stretch in your upper back.
• **BENEFITS** Releases back tension and massages the nerves that run down each side of the spine.

"The nerves up and down my spine are awakening"

Pull your knees towards your chest while keeping your back on the floor

1 Lie on your back with your knees bent. Clasp your hands under your knees, and pull your knees towards your chest.

Keep your hands clasped under your knees

2 Gently roll up to a sitting position. As this is part of a continuous rocking movement, balance on your buttocks, ready to rock back.

Try to touch your head with your knees

3 Roll backwards, lifting your back off the floor, and then roll up again. Repeat six times.

SPINE STRETCH

Imagine your legs, back, and neck are stretching as energy flows up your spine. Yogis believe this exercise stimulates the flow of spinal fluid.
• **BENEFITS** Stretches the ankles, legs, spine, and neck. Helps to prepare the body for the standing poses.

Flex your feet as you draw down your chin

Keep your arms at your sides throughout the exercise

1 Lie on your back. Draw your chin toward your chest, flexing your toes simultaneously.

"Energy flows up my spine"

Feel the stretch in your neck

2 Pull your chin up, arch the neck, and point your toes. Perform this stretch 12 times.

STANDING STRETCH

As you bend down, visualize all your muscles relaxing, and as you stretch up, imagine them lengthening to the limit.
• **BENEFITS** Cleans the lungs, stretches the back, legs, and upper torso. Also helps to reduce the stomach.

Bend your knees slightly

Try to touch the floor with your hands

1 Stand with your feet 50 cm (2 ft) apart, arms at sides. Bend your knees a little. Drop the top of your body down as far as is comfortable.

Straighten your knees as you stretch up

2 Stretch up, straightening your knees and inhaling. Drop down and exhale. Repeat at least ten times.

Keep your feet firmly on the floor

STANDING SWING

Visualize your body freely swinging as far as possible to each side. Feel your upper body loosening as you swing.
• **BENEFITS** Trims the waist and relaxes the neck muscles.

"My upper body is looser and my waist is trimmer"

Turn your head with your body

Twist your hips as you swing

The feet should be about 50 cm (2 ft) apart

With your arms extended and your feet firmly grounded, swing your body to one side, then the other. Repeat 20 times.

29

POLARITY STRETCH

Visualize the opposite poles of your body meeting in a stretch that extends from one end of the body to the other.

• **BENEFITS** Loosens the back, shoulders, and waist. Also improves circulation.

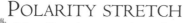

Feel the torso twist as you look at the extended hand

Stand with your feet 50 cm (2 ft) apart. Bend over with knees slightly bent and grasp your right ankle with your left hand. Extend your right arm up and behind you. Turn your head and look at the right hand. Hold for a count of six. Repeat on the other side. Now swing freely from side to side 14 times without clasping your ankles.

UPRIGHT LEG & HIP STRETCH

Visualize your weight centred in your hands. Rest your hands on the floor while you stretch upwards with your hips.

• **BENEFITS** Loosens the hip joints and ankles. Strengthens the back of the legs.

I Following the polarity stretch, bend your knees and drop your body down. Place your hands hip-width apart between your feet.

Squat low with your weight centred in your hands

2 Tap your left elbow with your left knee. Alternating sides, repeat 20 times in total.

3 Walk your hands forward and slowly straighten your knees. Then walk your feet in towards your hands. Stand up slowly.

Make a fist and balance on your knuckles for ease

PELVIC ARCH

Visualize the muscles of your thighs, lower back, and stomach holding your entire spine in a graceful relaxing arch.

• **BENEFITS** Strengthens the back, stomach, and thighs. Also tones the pelvic area.

Contract your buttocks to support your thighs and hips

Lie down with your arms at your sides and your knees bent. Push your pelvis upwards to form an arch. Hold for a count of ten, and then allow your pelvis to return to the floor. Repeat six times.

FLOOR FLYING

Visualize yourself flying through space with your arms and legs extended, and your entire body energized by the spine.
• **BENEFITS** Strengthens the back.

Lie with your arms above your head. Raise your head, chest, arms, and legs for a count of ten. Spread your arms to your sides like wings and hold for ten seconds. Return your arms to the front, hold for another ten seconds, release, and relax.

Stretch your raised legs and arms

SHOULDER STAND

(Exclude if you have a back or neck problem.) Visualize your organs, normally weighed down by gravity, returning to their proper place.
• **BENEFITS** Stimulates the thyroid gland, feeds the head with blood, and rests the internal organs.

1 Lie on your back with your knees bent. Raise your legs and push your back off the floor.

2 Push your body upwards, your back supported by your hands. Keep moving your body up until you are on resting on your shoulders. Tuck your chin into your chest.

Press the palms of your hands on the floor to help raise your back

Gradually straighten your legs

"My internal organs are falling into place"

Keep your back straight, supported by your hands

Make sure that your neck is comfortable

3 You should be balanced on and supported by your shoulders, and your neck should feel comfortable. Stay in this position for about one to two minutes, or for as long as you feel comfortable. Bend your knees and roll gently onto your back.

SURRENDER STRETCH

You are letting go of all mental and physical tension. Completely surrender to your inner energy.
• **BENEFITS** Stretches the upper and lower back and the arms, and tightens the stomach. Yogis believe that pressure on the forehead promotes a confident attitude.

Lie on your stomach with your arms bent and your hands positioned beside your shoulders. Push your body up into a kneeling position with your hands and arms, and with your legs spread apart. Slide your arms forward and drop your head down until it reaches the ground. Try to hold this position for 20 seconds.

Feel the stretch along your back

"I surrender to my inner energy"

Your forehead should touch the floor

BACK-OF-LEG STRETCH

Visualize your spine elongating as you extend your leg and neck. Feel the integration of your limbs and body.
• **BENEFITS** Stretches the back and legs. Also slims and firms the buttocks and thighs.

Touch your head with your knee

1 Kneel on your hands and knees. Lift up your right leg and swing the knee towards your head.

"I feel the stretch in my spine"

As you extend your leg, lift it as high as possible

2 Extend your right leg, point your toes, and raise your head and neck. Perform 12 times on one leg, then change legs and repeat.

LEG LIFT

Visualize the pelvis pushing into the floor, the legs strong and straight.
• **BENEFITS** Stimulates the adrenals, tones the pelvic area, strengthens the back, and stretches the hamstrings.

Keep the raised leg as straight as possible

HAND POSITION
Make each hand into a fist, and place near the top of the thighs.

1 Lie flat on your stomach with your fists under your groin. Lift your right leg and raise your head and chest. Put your weight on your right fist. Hold for ten seconds. Release. Repeat with the left leg.

Support your pelvis on your fists

2 Lift both legs, pushing your pelvis into your fists. At the same time, lift up your head and chest. Holding this position, take 20–30 rapid breaths.

CAT STRETCH

Visualize yourself as a languid cat stretching its entire spine. (Consider how animals conserve their energy by totally relaxing, expending energy only when absolutely necessary.)
• **BENEFITS** Stretches the spine and stimulates the intestines. Also benefits the central nervous system.

"I am as powerful as a jungle cat"

Raise your back into a hump with your head down

Ease your back into a concave shape

1 Kneel on your hands and knees with your back straight. Lower your head. Inhale and curve your back into a hump with your stomach pulled in.

2 Assume the reverse position with your head and tailbone up. Push your stomach toward the floor. Repeat this sequence six times.

AROMATHERAPY

THE ART AND SCIENCE of aromatherapy – treatment with fragrance – began thousands of years ago and is now undergoing a modern revival as we seek more natural ways to reduce stress, relieve aches and pains, improve skin, and lift our spirits. Essential oils from plants, flowers, and trees, such as rosemary, sandalwood, and

SCENTED OILS

lavender, are the wonder-workers of aromatherapy. They are responsible for its unique ability to deliver the ultimate in sensory health and pleasure. Hands-on application of essential oils in a massage especially designed to deliver their benefits is an experience that has come to be appreciated around the world. Fragrances can make us feel lively or relaxed, soulful or sexy, depending on the essences used, since

COMFORTABLE CUSHIONS

our olfactory sense, or sense of smell, communicates odour messages to our entire being, affecting the way we think and feel. Also, the skin is able to absorb essential oils, reinforcing the olfactory impact. With the right ambience and careful selection of the appropriate essential oils and their correct and sensitive application, you can transform a standard massage, facial, or bath into a sensory epiphany. Aromatherapy is the alchemy of bliss.

SOFT TOWELS

PARTNER MASSAGE

*Caring touch combined with pure natural essential oils
has a profound effect on the psyche and the body.*

MASSAGE DETOXIFIES and relaxes the body. As you stroke upwards, body toxins are directed along the lymph system – a network of veins and capillaries – into the lymph nodes for purification, while the sensitive touch of a partner relaxes the body and soothes the mind.

Partner massage is a shared experience. The person who performs the massage is giving, the individual receiving is open and trusting. Create the perfect atmosphere by scenting the air with the same essences you plan to use in the massage, dimming the lights, and playing soothing music. Your touch should be warm but sensitive. Be aware of the body as you massage, and especially any physical problem.

Do not massage anyone who has had an operation recently, or has heart disease, open sores, swellings, or a fever. Varicose veins should be avoided. Massage pregnant women only lightly, and with mild floral or fruit oils.

THE BASIC STROKES

*The three simple strokes shown below are the basis
of most partner massage movements.*

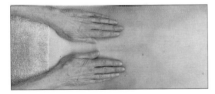

◄ EFFLEURAGE
This long sweeping stroke relaxes and encourages lymphatic and blood flow. Use your entire palm and fingers as you stroke, curving slightly around the body's contours.

ACUPRESSURE ►
Lay the whole hand on the body but apply pressure just with the thumbs. Use this stroke along nerve pathways such as those on either side of the spine. Put weight behind each pressure.

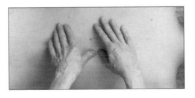

◄ PETRISSAGE (KNEADING)
Press the flesh with the fingers and thumbs of both hands as if you are kneading bread. This firm kneading stroke helps to relieve tense muscles and improve circulation.

HOW TO BEGIN
Wash your hands, and be sure your fingernails are short and will not scratch the skin. Essential oils are powerful and must be used with great respect. Pour a small amount of oil into the palm of one hand. Lightly rub your hands together and begin the massage.

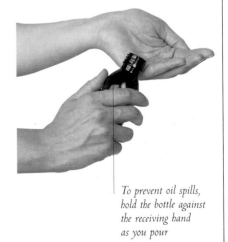

To prevent oil spills, hold the bottle against the receiving hand as you pour

BACK~OF~BODY MASSAGE

Perform the massage on a bed or a sturdy table. Ask the person you are massaging to lie face-down. Cover the entire body, except the area you are to massage, with towels.

PREPARATION
Before you begin the massage, shake your hands to release any tension that they may be holding. Take a deep breath and focus on the gift you are about to give.

Place a rolled towel or small pillow under the ankles to relieve the lower back

FIGURE OF EIGHT

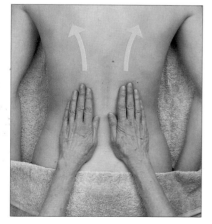

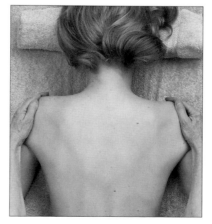

1 This is the first stroke of a lightly pressured effleurage movement that covers the entire back. Begin with your hands at the top of the buttocks. Then sweep them upwards along each side of the spine.

2 When you reach the shoulders, curve your hands over and around them. The stroke should be part of a continuous sweeping movement.

3 Run your hands down the sides of the back. Cross your hands at the middle of the back, and bring them up the sides of the buttocks. Repeat the entire figure-of-eight sequence five times.

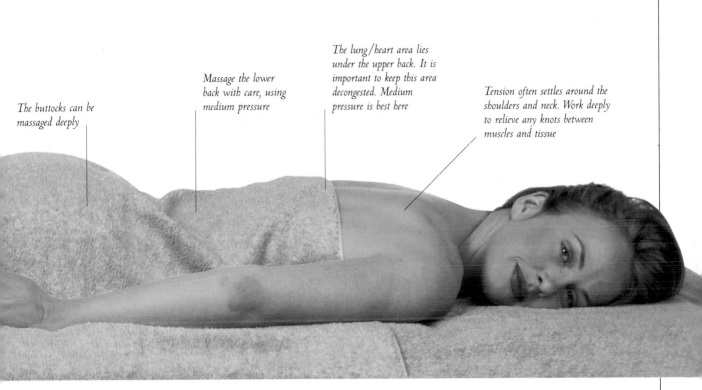

The buttocks can be massaged deeply

Massage the lower back with care, using medium pressure

The lung/heart area lies under the upper back. It is important to keep this area decongested. Medium pressure is best here

Tension often settles around the shoulders and neck. Work deeply to relieve any knots between muscles and tissue

THUMB PRESSURES

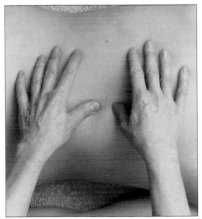

4 Stimulate the central nervous system with these pressures. Place your thumbs at the base of the spine, along one side. Move up to the neck along the spine with gentle pressures. Perform five times on alternate sides.

BACK SWEEPS

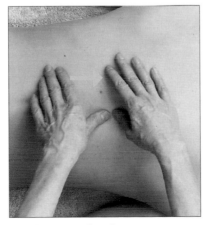

5 Place your thumbs tip-to-tip at the base of one side of the spine. Sweep your thumbs up to the neck three times. Repeat on the other side. Perform five times on alternate sides.

BACK SCOOPS

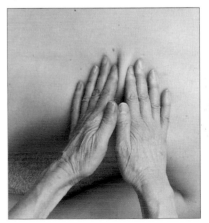

6 Starting at one buttock, lift up the back tissue between straight fingers. Work up one side to the neck. Return to the other buttock and repeat the process. Perform three times on each side of the spine.

BACK SWEEPS

7 Place your hands on one side of the spine. Slide them to the table and then return them to the spine. Move up the spine and repeat the stroke. Repeat three times on each side of the spine.

KIDNEY SWEEPS

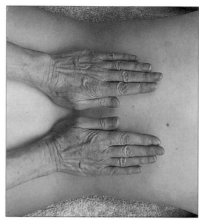

8 Place your hands on the back, just above the hips. Sweep upwards with short, brisk strokes. Each stroke should be 30 cm (12 in) long. This stroke flushes the kidneys and stimulates the adrenal glands.

BACK KNEADING

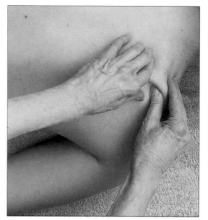

9 Work from the outer shoulder inwards, kneading the tissue. Slide both hands from the inside of the shoulder blade over the shoulder and around in a circular motion six times. Repeat on the other shoulder.

BACK-OF-LEG SWEEPS

Begin and finish the sequence of leg sweeps with your hands held against the feet

10 These leg sweeps encourage lymphatic drainage. Begin by firmly holding your hands on the soles of the feet for ten seconds.

Rest the calves on a soft bolster or rolled-up towel

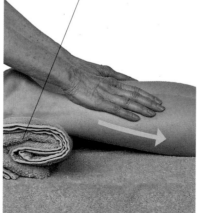

11 Move your hands onto the ankles, and clasp them firmly for ten seconds. Stroke them in a circular motion with your fingers. Then run the palms of your hands up the calves.

Keep your hands flat as you sweep up the legs

12 Sweep up the centre of the legs to the outer thighs using moderate pressure. Repeat three times from the ankles to the outer thighs. Finish with your hands firmly held against the feet for 20 seconds.

FRONT~OF~BODY MASSAGE

*Since your partner may feel more vulnerable when he or she turns over and
exposes the front of the body, immediately cover it with the towel.*

PREPARATION
*Place a towel or pillow under the knees
for comfort. Wash your hands since you
will be massaging the head first.*

*Massage the stomach with
sensitivity. Use a clockwise
circling motion to work in
the same direction as the
ascending colon*

*The head should be lying
flat on the table, centred
between the shoulders*

*Use upward sweeps
rather than deep massage
on these bony areas*

HEAD PRESSURES

I Start by holding your hands
gently on each side of the head
for a few seconds. Press the head
with your thumbs, moving at 2.5 cm
(1 in) intervals from the top of the
forehead to the back of the head.

DEEP SHOULDER RELIEF

*Press firmly
with your
thumb*

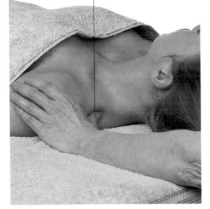

*Use all your fingers
to massage the
shoulders*

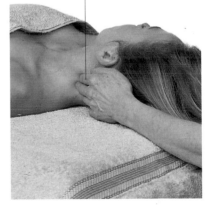

2 Shoulder muscles are often tight,
and require firm pressure. Turn
the head to one side. With your
thumb, press from the end of one
shoulder up to the back of the neck.

3 Reach under the head and, using
a circular motion, massage the
base of the skull with all your fingers
for a couple of minutes. Perform this
firm shoulder-to-skull massage three
times on each shoulder.

SHOULDER PUSH

4 Curve your hands around the shoulders and push down, then release twice on the outside edges. This stroke relaxes the shoulders and stimulates lymphatic drainage in the neck and chest.

CHEST PUMPS

5 From the collarbone, slide your hands down the centre of the chest. Stop at the top of the breast and apply pressure with a quick pumping motion. Repeat once.

UNDER SHOULDERS

6 Slide your hands underneath the shoulders, close to the spine. From here, massage the shoulder blades, upper back, and shoulders with a firm circular stroke. Rest your arms on the table for comfort.

ARM SWEEPS

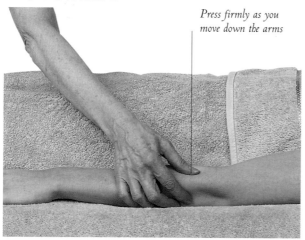

Press firmly as you move down the arms

7 Place both your hands side by side under the collarbone, and simultaneously sweep them outwards to the outside of the shoulder. Press firmly into the outside of the shoulder, middle arm, and top of wrists, then sweep out to the ends of the fingers. Repeat the entire movement three times.

FINGER MASSAGE

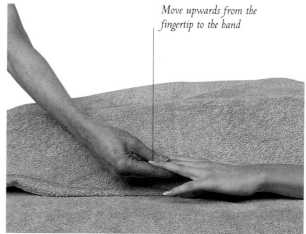

Move upwards from the fingertip to the hand

8 As you finish the last finger sweep, take each finger into your fingers and massage from tip to hand. Turn the hand over and massage the palm. Complete the movement by sweeping up the arm to the shoulder. Repeat the sequence on the other hand.

ENERGIZING THE SOLAR PLEXUS

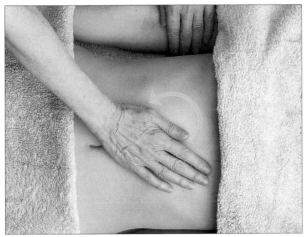

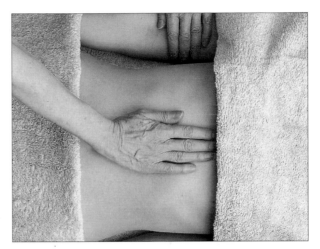

9 The solar plexus, or diaphragm, is a repository of nerve and muscle. Exponents of yoga believe that it is a source of great energy. Hold the right arm with your left hand. With your right hand, gently stroke the solar plexus in an anti-clockwise motion just below the breast-bone. Circle six times.

10 When you have completed the circling motion, hold your hand still on the solar plexus and send positive messages to the person you are massaging. This action is very soothing and centring.

FRONT LEG SWEEPS

Keep the movement upwards to facilitate lymphatic drainage

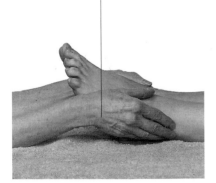

11 Hold the palms of your hands against the soles of the feet for five seconds. Slide them to the ankles. Hold for two seconds. Slide up to the knee, and hold. Move to the thighs and off the leg. Repeat three times.

FEET SWEEPS

Use a firm pressure as you run your thumbs from heel to toes

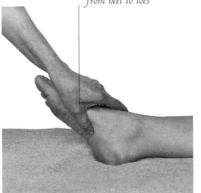

12 Grasp the top of the feet and press your thumbs on the heels. Run the thumbs up the feet, from heels to toes. Pull the end of each toe, starting with the big toe.

FINISHING OFF

Hold the palm of your hand flat against the foot

13 To finish, once again press your hands against the feet for 20 seconds. Place towels over any exposed areas of the person you have massaged. Let him or her rest for a few minutes before sitting up.

SELF~MASSAGE

The stimulation of your own hand, combined with the effect of essential oils, can be just as effective as being massaged by a partner.

HELP YOURSELF relax with this simple self-massage. You should be able to reach almost every part of your face and body, with the exception of your middle back.

The best time to give yourself this uplifting experience is after a bath, when you are warm and relaxed. Prepare the room with as much care as if you were having a partner massage. Either sit on a stool or massage yourself while sitting on cushions on the floor. Dim the lights, and either burn incense or heat essential oils to scent the air. Play dreamy music to enhance the sensual effect. Take a few deep breaths and relax. Pour a small amount of oil into your hands and sweep it onto the first area to be massaged. Inhale the mood-making fragrance, and allow yourself to be transported by the music as you stroke and knead your body.

BODY MASSAGE

Restore every cell in your body with a magical self~massage. Increase flexibility, improve circulation, and release tension with these simple strokes.

Begin the stroke at the base of one side of the neck

Sweep outwards from collarbone to armpits

Curve your hand around your arm and squeeze

1 Knead firmly from the base of one side of your neck outwards to the top of your arm and back. Repeat six times on each side.

2 Using all fingers, sweep with a firm action underneath the centre of the collarbone to your armpits. Repeat this detoxifying movement 12 times.

3 To help circulation, firmly knead the arm from wrist to shoulder, using the opposite hand. Repeat six times on each arm.

4 Rest your leg on a stool or chair. Place your hands on the ankle and work up to the knee, stroking firmly with the hands. Stroke six times on one leg, and repeat on the other.

Work upwards to encourage lymphatic drainage

5 In a continuation of the previous step, run your hands over your knee to the top of the thigh. Use both hands, keeping the effleurage movement firm but fluid.

The thigh muscle is large and dense, so work deeply here

HAND MASSAGE

These strokes improve finger flexibility. Work each hand for three minutes.

1 Grasp one hand with the opposite hand and, using thumb and fingers, massage the palm and back of the hand with a firm circular motion.

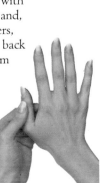

2 Firmly squeeze each finger from base to fingertip. Work in small circular movements. Repeat on other hand.

FOOT MASSAGE

Soak your feet in scented water. Dry and apply oil. Work each foot for five minutes.

1 Massage upwards on each sole from toe to ankle, pressing firmly with your thumb.

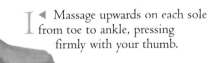

2 Finish the foot massage by grasping each toe and firmly massaging to its tip.

FACIAL MASSAGE

*Always stroke your face gently,
moving upwards and outwards.
Pressure can be firm,
but never pull the
facial skin.*

Massage the oil
into the skin with
your fingertips

Tap as if you
are playing a
keyboard

1 Apply a small amount of facial oil, which should contain mild floral essence *(see p.49)*. Gently massage the oil into your skin with your fingertips, working in small circles in an outwards direction.

2 Tap firmly across your forehead and down your face with the fingertips of both hands. Repeat several times. This movement helps oil absorption and head and face circulation. You are literally waking up nerve endings.

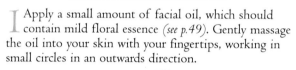

Slide two fingers from
the centre of your
forehead outwards

Pinch with
the thumb and
index finger

3 The forehead slide has a very soothing effect, and can help to relieve stress-induced headaches. Place two fingers of both hands on the centre of your forehead, and slide them firmly towards the temples. Repeat six times.

4 With your thumb and index finger, pinch along the eyebrow. Move from the centre of the forehead outwards. After three eyebrow pressures, make a circle with your fingertips over your closed eye. Repeat six times.

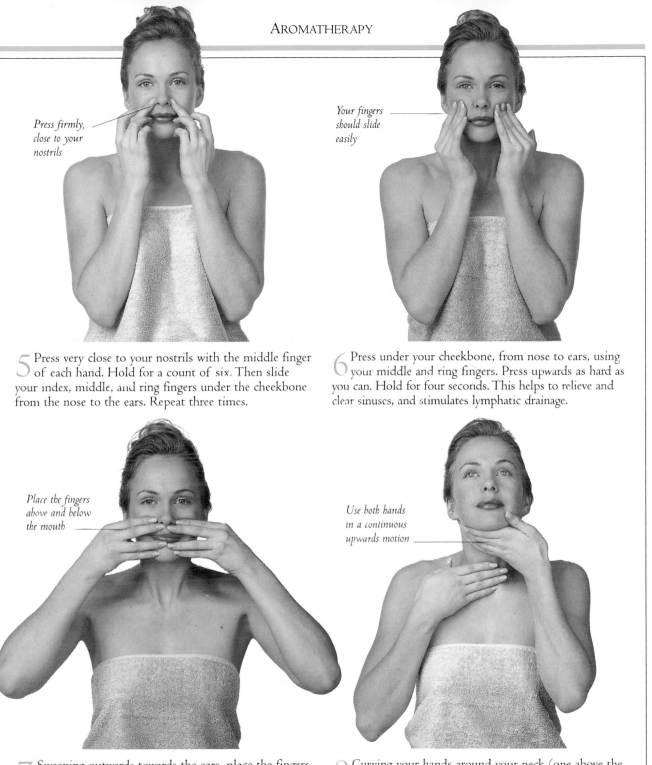

Press firmly, close to your nostrils

Your fingers should slide easily

5 Press very close to your nostrils with the middle finger of each hand. Hold for a count of six. Then slide your index, middle, and ring fingers under the cheekbone from the nose to the ears. Repeat three times.

6 Press under your cheekbone, from nose to ears, using your middle and ring fingers. Press upwards as hard as you can. Hold for four seconds. This helps to relieve and clear sinuses, and stimulates lymphatic drainage.

Place the fingers above and below the mouth

Use both hands in a continuous upwards motion

7 Sweeping outwards towards the ears, place the fingers of both hands above and below the mouth, covering the area from under the cheekbone to the chin. This movement clears the facial lymph into nodes in the neck.

8 Curving your hands around your neck (one above the other on each side), sweep upwards from the collarbone to the chin. As you stroke upwards, move from the side to the front of the side of your neck. Repeat ten times.

AROMATHERAPY BATHING

Bathing in water scented with essential oils is a sensory pleasure that is also beneficial to your health. The experience will invigorate or calm, depending on which oils you use.

IN AN AROMATHERAPY bath or shower, the action of the essential oils is enhanced by the warm water and its vapour. The fragrance is delivered to your olfactory system by steam and through the skin which, softened by the warm water, quickly absorbs the essences.

If you lack energy, pick yourself up with an energizing bath or shower. Use an invigorating essence such as rosemary to add to your bathwater, or use a shower gel with added essential oils. Give your body a dry-brush massage and then immerse yourself in a tub of lukewarm, not hot, water. Massage your limbs and torso under water. Rinse with cool or cold water. Then slap yourself dry from feet to neck with

both hands. Finish drying yourself with a towel. Massage an energizing oil, such as juniper or geranium, into your skin.

For a calming bath, diffuse lavender into the air, draw a very warm bath, and add a mixture of lavender and vetiver to the bathwater. Sink into the bath and let go. Soak for ten minutes and dry with a towel. Afterwards, massage a mixture of basil and clary sage into your skin.

For a luxurious bath, light candles, diffuse an exotic fragrance into the air, and play soothing music. Scent your bathwater with a sensuous essence, such as patchouli. Lie in the bath, close your eyes, inhale the essences, and revel in the blissful warmth of the water.

Relax by closing your eyes and breathing deeply to inhale the scented air

A scent warmer will fill the air with fragrance as well as give a gentle light

BATHING TECHNIQUES

*To receive the most from your aromatherapy bathing, use
these simple techniques before and after the experience.*

DRY BRUSHING

Treating the skin with a dry brush
removes dead cells and cleans pores,
preparing the skin for bathing or
massage. Buy a brush made for the
purpose – a natural bristle brush
is best. Brush upwards from
feet to neck, but exclude
any sensitive areas.

*Brush your skin in
a circular motion*

SLAPPING DRY

When your body is still wet from
your bath or shower, vigorously
slap yourself dry. Work from the
arms, to the torso and down the
legs to the feet. Finish by rubbing
briskly with a textured towel.
You will feel alive, and your
skin will be glowing.

*Stimulate your
skin by slapping
dry with the palm
of your hand*

PREPARING THE BATH

*Run the water into the bath. Add your choice of essential
oil mixture when the bath is half full. If you add the
essence to the hot water as it first flows into the bath,
some of the fragrance will evaporate before you benefit
from its full impact when sitting in the water.*

*Place soft towels
nearby. Warm them
for extra comfort*

SETTING THE SCENE

Transform even the most ordinary
bathroom into an inviting spa with
gentle lighting, soothing music, and
aromatic essences. Enjoy the height
of luxury by sprinkling a few fragrant
rose petals in the bath. And have a
soft, thick towel waiting for you.

AROMATHERAPY OILS

Every essential oil has a specific effect on the mind and body as it penetrates the skin and sense of smell. The following formulas utilize the individual properties of a readily available selection of essential oils.

THE RECIPES I suggest opposite give the oil combinations that you can use for particular conditions, such as headaches, stress, or water retention. I also explain how you apply them: on the face or body as massage oils, as bath or shower oils, or as room fragrances. Although most of the essences are suitable for all these functions (in different quantities), the face always requires very gentle formulations.

Essential oils are very powerful and must always be mixed with a base oil before you use them. The correct proportion of essential oil to base oil required for various types of massage oils is explained opposite. Apricot kernel, sesame, avocado, and wheat germ oils are all good, nourishing base oils for the face. Apply them alone or in combination. For the body, combine sesame, apricot kernel, jojoba, and sweet almond to make an excellent base oil. I use this mix for my own product line with excellent results. For bath or shower preparations, mix the essential oil of your choice with one teaspoon of mild Castile or baby shampoo. This will disperse the essence into the water. Never put essential oils directly into the bathwater. They do not mix well with the water and float on top, where a particularly strong essence can be irritating to the skin. It is difficult to make your own shower gel, but you can buy some effective premixed ones with little fragrance, and then boost them with essences. Alternatively, you can add essential oils to a soft liquid soap. Use an inert oil, such as mineral oil, to make a room fragrance. Since most diffusers heat the oils to disperse them into the air, avoid base oils that smoke or burn and so ruin the fragrance. Make sure that all your essential oils are fresh and stored tightly sealed, away from heat and light.

STORING OILS
Keep your oils in opaque, airtight bottles. If you want to display them, decant what you need for a few days into clear glass bottles.

AROMATHERAPY RECIPES

The following formulas are calculated for one massage, bath, or shower, or
for scenting one medium-sized room. Choose a base oil from page 48,
and check the ratio of base oil to essence in the box below.

ANXIETY
Basil & Clary Sage *or* Vetiver & Lavender
Rub on wrists and solar plexus • Inhale

ARTHRITIS & MUSCULAR ACHES
Arnica & Juniper *or* Eucalyptus & Rosemary
Massage into affected areas • Add to bath water

DEPRESSION
Basil & Clary Sage *or* Marjoram & Ylang-ylang
Rub on wrists, temples, and solar plexus
Inhale • Add to bath water

OEDEMA (WATER RETENTION)
Juniper & Lemon *or* Sandalwood & Lavender
Massage on affected areas • Add to bath water

FATIGUE & EXHAUSTION
Juniper & Lemon *or* Rosemary & Geranium
Massage over entire body • Add to bath water

FEMALE PROBLEMS, MENSTRUAL CRAMPS, MENOPAUSE
Cypress & Lavender *or* Chamomile & Sage
Massage over entire body • Add to bath water

HEADACHE
Peppermint & Chamomile *or*
Lavender & Rosemary
Rub on wrists and temples • Inhale
Add to bath water

INDIGESTION & GAS
Basil & Chamomile *or* Fennel & Peppermint
Massage over abdomen
Add to bath water

NERVOUS TENSION & STRESS
Lavender & Vetiver *or* Chamomile & Rose
Massage over solar plexus • Inhale • Add to bath water

SINUS PROBLEMS
Eucalyptus & Pine *or* Cypress & Niaouli
Inhale • Add to bath water

SKIN DRYNESS & IRRITATIONS
Lavender & Patchouli *or* Sandalwood & Rose
Massage over entire body • Add to bath water

SENSUALITY
Sandalwood & Patchouli *or* Sandalwood & Rose
Massage over entire body • Inhale • Add to bath water

TOXICITY
Lavender & Cypress *or* Juniper & Lemon
Massage over entire body • Add to bath water

FACIAL MASSAGE: DRY & MATURE SKIN
Chamomile & Rose *or* Sandalwood & Patchouli

FACIAL MASSAGE: NORMAL SKIN
Lavender & Chamomile *or* Lavender & Rosewood

FACIAL MASSAGE: OILY SKIN
Lavender & Lemon *or* Geranium & Chamomile

QUANTITY OF ESSENTIAL OIL TO BASE
MASSAGE • 2 drops each essence in 30 ml (1 fl oz) base oil
FACE • 1 drop each essence in 15 ml (½ fl oz) base oil
BATH • 4 drops each essence in 1 teaspoon shampoo
SHOWER • 2 drops each essence in 1 tablespoon liquid soap
ROOM • 3 drops each essence in 1 teaspoon base oil

SENSORY FOOD

FOOD CREATES and supports the life force in all that exists on the earth and in its surrounding seas. Take away food and nothing else matters because nothing lives. Critical as it is to our existence, we take food for granted. It is readily available in shops and restaurants, and most of us can feed ourselves with relative ease. Convenience, however, does not necessarily

FRESH PRODUCE

mean health and satisfaction. Without much effort, we can receive more in a healthy way from food. All we have to do is to use our senses to become aware of the food that we eat.

In the 5th century BC, the Greek physician Hippocrates used plants and other natural food-based remedies to cure maladies and to build health. A plant-based natural diet

QUALITY OILS & VINEGARS

supplies the vitamins, minerals, carbohydrates, and proteins that our bodies were created to assimilate. Studies of the world's healthiest people show that their diets consist mainly of locally grown grains and vegetables, which are naturally low in fat and high in fibre. So we should look for the freshest food that is in its most whole, preferably organic, state. Always try to eat the real thing. Fooling with food is foolish.

VITAMIN-RICH FOOD

SHOPPING

Most of us shop for food as if it were just another commodity, making our selection on the basis of need and price, rather than on quality. This has become especially true since the establishment of vast supermarkets.

LET'S PLAY a game. The next time you are in your supermarket, allow the fresh produce to talk to you. Strike up a silent conversation and ask the food how fresh and flavoursome it is, and whether it has been doused by chemicals. When you start to do this, you will establish a new relationship with what you buy.

When I look at a display of oranges, the shape, colour, aroma, and texture of certain oranges "speak" to me. When I feel that a particular orange has my name on it, it goes into my basket. If I do this, I find that I enjoy the orange more. Try it. Turn on your food focus and use your senses to make your choices. If possible, smell any food before you buy. Your nose was meant to detect freshness. Check for living colour. Give produce a gentle squeeze to make sure it's firm and crisp. The look, smell, feel-good test should help assure maximum nutrition and taste.

COOKING & EATING

Great chefs are truly absorbed in the food they prepare. They taste, feel, smell, and listen to the food they cook. This heightened sensitivity is what makes the difference between ordinary and gourmet cuisine. It can also help to produce food that is more nutritious as well as delicious.

PREPARATION IS all-important. Good stainless steel cooking utensils will help your cooking, as well as preserve the vitamins, minerals, and flavours of the food you cook. A steamer is a must for vegetables; if you boil roots and greens in water, most of their vitamins and minerals will be lost. Wash, peel, and chop fruits and vegetables just before you use them. This will prevent oxidation (the destruction of plant cells by oxygen) and nutrient loss.

Always use the best ingredients, including the best oils, herbs, and spices. Every ingredient makes a difference to the taste, aroma, and colour of the finished dish. Food that looks good will taste better. Serving food is an art that fully engages the senses. Try to arrange your food decoratively on the plate and find time to dress the table attractively with mats, linens, flowers, and special lighting. Do this even if you are dining alone, or especially if you are alone, for a decorative dinner will lift your spirits if they are low.

We have an intimate relationship with nature through the food that we eat. As we bite, chew, and swallow, we are literally taking part of our universe into ourselves.

COOKING WITH YOUR SENSES

Let your mouth, nose, and eyes lead you to culinary excellence as you cook and dine.

▼ PREPARATION
Wash your hands before preparing food, and handle it with love. Be aware of your nurturing role as food provider for yourself, friends, and family.

▲ INGREDIENTS
High-quality, unprocessed food is an investment that pays off in increased energy, glowing skin, and pleasure. Pay a little more for the finest and freshest.

▲ PRESENTATION
Entice the eyes as well as the palate with colour-balanced meals. Make a salad with a range of leaf textures and colours, for example.

We should take this seriously and realize that it can feed the soul as well as the stomach if the senses are fully involved. Your olfactory response is particularly important to your enjoyment of food. The way food smells will affect the way it tastes to you. Also, it is a good idea to play relaxing music while you eat. This will help your digestive juices to flow more rhythmically, and you will probably take more time to chew each bite. Fifty per cent of our digestion takes place in the mouth. (Remember, you have no teeth in your stomach!)

Overeating strains both digestion and assimilation. The stomach can comfortably cope with about two cups of food at any one time. Beyond that, most of what you eat is undigested, and undigested food creates toxic residue. Your golden rule for food should be "more nutritional value and less quantity in one meal".

A FEAST FOR THE SENSES
Smell, gaze upon, and taste your food before you eat it. Chew slowly, savouring every bite. Note all the different sensations produced by the tastes and smells of the ingredients.

DINING WITH YOUR SENSES

Your senses of sight, taste, and smell turn on your entire digestive system and pleasure (and pain) centres.

Your sensory perception of what you eat is critical to how much it benefits you. Social conditioning and habit play an important role in your visual, olfactory, and flavour response to food. Go beyond this and develop an appreciation for food that is real and natural. Enjoy the knowledge that this type of food is benefiting you.

TRUE TASTE
Our taste buds become jaded with years of overseasoning and cooking with too much fat. If a salad is drowned in dressing, you will never know the subtle taste of fresh crisp lettuces. Go for 48 hours without salt, and see how salty everything tastes afterwards.

RECIPES

If you enjoy eating, it's convenient to enjoy cooking. I happen to like both. The following recipes have been tested in my kitchen and enthusiastically consumed by me, my family, and my guests for many years. A tip I recently learned is that you should never serve food too hot or too cold. In both cases, you kill the taste. Always allow refrigerated fruits and vegetables to reach room temperature before eating them.

VEGETABLE JUICES

Freshly extracted vegetable juice is more than nutritious, it is therapeutic. When certain vegetable juices are combined they produce a natural chemistry that can detoxify and heal. For this reason, it is better to allow at least 30 minutes for the particular formula you are drinking to be digested before eating other food. Be sure you use fresh, thoroughly washed vegetables. Consume the juice immediately after extraction and drink slowly to aid absorption. Use a juice extractor for these recipes. All juice recipes make a single serving.

CARROT & CELERY JUICE

High in beta-carotene, carrots are good for eyes and skin. Celery is high in sodium, which keeps calcium fluid.

INGREDIENTS
2 celery stalks • 3 large carrots

Wash and chop the celery stalks and carrots. Process the celery first, add the carrots, and then process the mixture.

MINERAL COCKTAIL

This formula cleanses the digestive tract and encourages waste elimination.

INGREDIENTS
4 spinach leaves • 3 parsley sprigs 2 celery stalks • 3 large carrots

Wash and chop the vegetables. Process the spinach, parsley, and celery. Add the carrots and then process the mixture.

CARROT, BEETROOT, & CUCUMBER JUICE

A super cleanser for the gall bladder, liver, kidneys, and sexual glands.

INGREDIENTS
2 beetroot leaves • ½ medium cucumber • 1 beetroot • 4 carrots

Wash and chop the vegetables. Process the beetroot leaves and cucumber. Add the beetroot and carrots and process the mixture.

BREAKFAST

Breakfast stimulates our senses of taste and smell and awakens our appetite for the new day. Introducing nourishing comfort food can get our psyche and digestion off to the right start. Chew well, and enjoy every morsel.

MORNING MILLET

Millet is an easily digested grain. It is high in protein, calcium, B vitamins, and lecithin, and has a mild, slightly sweet flavour.

INGREDIENTS

*160 g (6 oz) hulled millet • 1 tbsp chopped dried apricots
1 tbsp sultanas • pinch sea salt • ¼ tsp nutmeg
2 tbsp toasted, flaked almonds*

Preheat the oven to 150°C/300°F/Gas 2. Combine the millet with 500 ml (16 fl oz) of boiling water. Add the apricots, sultanas, salt, and nutmeg. Pour into a baking dish and cover. Bake in the oven for 40 minutes. Serve topped with toasted almonds. Millet is delicious served with milk and with maple syrup or honey. Almond milk (made in a blender from almonds and water with a drop of vanilla) offers a healthy alternative to cow's milk. *Serves 2–3*

NUTTY BANANA MUFFINS

A delicious complement to a fruit and yogurt breakfast, these muffins are packed with energizing grains, natural sugars, and fibre.

INGREDIENTS

1 egg • 2 medium-ripe mashed bananas • 80 ml (3 fl oz) vegetable oil • 3 tbsp honey • 60 ml (2 fl oz) yogurt • 150 g (5 oz) whole wheat flour • 60 g (2 oz) wheat germ • 70 g (2½ oz) chopped walnuts • ½ tsp bicarbonate of soda • ½ tsp baking powder • ½ tsp ground cinnamon • ½ tsp ground mace

Preheat the oven to 180°C/350°F/Gas 4. Oil a 12-cup muffin pan. Beat the egg. Add the bananas, oil, honey, and yogurt. In another bowl, mix the dry ingredients. Add to the liquid ingredients and stir. Pour the batter into the muffin pan. Bake for 25 minutes. Cool. *Makes 12*

JUDITH'S GRANOLA

Oats are rich in fibre and B vitamins. Nuts and seeds contain high-quality protein, and are a source of magnesium and vitamin E. All nuts and seeds should be raw.

INGREDIENTS

*450 g (1 lb) organic oats • 100 g (4 oz) almonds
50 g (2 oz) pecan halves • 50 g (2 oz) Brazil nuts
80 g (3 oz) sunflower seeds • 60 ml (2 fl oz) sesame oil
60 ml (2 fl oz) maple syrup or honey
25 g (1 oz) dried, unsweetened, shredded coconut*

Preheat the oven to 140°C/275°F/Gas 1. Mix the oats in a bowl with the coarsely chopped nuts and the seeds. Warm the oil and mix in the syrup or honey. Pour slowly over the oats. Mix well. Spread over two shallow baking pans. Toast in the oven for 45 minutes. Empty the granola into your original bowl. Add the coconut while the granola mixture is still warm, and then allow to cool. This cereal is especially good served with a ripe banana. Soya, rice, or nut milks are also delicious with granola. *Serves 8*

MAIN COURSES

These main courses are often meals in themselves and work well for lunch or dinner. I've paid particular attention to sensory satisfaction, so savour the naturally delicious flavours by inhaling deeply and chewing well.

GRILLED CHICKEN SALAD WITH CURRIED MAYONNAISE

Chicken is a good source of protein. The greens provide vitamin A and calcium.

INGREDIENTS

2 free-range chicken breasts without skin • 2 tsp sesame or vegetable oil • 1 tsp chopped fresh rosemary • ½ tsp curry powder ¼ tsp mustard powder • 100 ml (4 fl oz) low-fat mayonnaise 1 bunch rocket • 4 leaves radicchio • 1 chicory head 150 g (5 oz) cherry tomatoes • a few sprigs of watercress salt and freshly ground black pepper

Preheat grill to High. Rub chicken breasts with oil and rosemary. Grill for 7–8 minutes on each side until cooked. Allow to cool. Add the curry powder and mustard powder to the mayonnaise. Toss salad greens with half of the mayonnaise. Arrange salad on two plates, top with chicken breasts, and garnish with tomatoes and watercress. Season. Serve the remaining mayonnaise on the side. *Serves 2*

VEGETABLE SOUP

This is hot, nourishing, and low in calories. It is high in potassium and other minerals.

INGREDIENTS

3 carrots • 2 potatoes • 2 onions • 4 celery stalks 2 tbsp vegetable oil • 1 litre (1¾ pints) vegetable stock sea salt and pepper • 100 g (3½ oz) green beans 100 g (3½ oz) butter beans • 100 g (3½ oz) peas

Wash, peel, and chop the carrots, potatoes, and onions. Wash and chop the celery. Sauté the onion until soft. Add carrots, potatoes, celery, stock, and seasoning. Boil, then simmer for 20 minutes. Add the green beans, butter beans, and peas, and cook for another 10 minutes. *Serves 2*

REJUVENATION SALAD

This is a satisfying luncheon salad that nourishes the skin, and combats ageing oxidants with vitamins A and E from the greens, beta-carotene from the carrot, and vitamin A and potassium from the apple.

INGREDIENTS

1 large apple, cut into bite-sized pieces • 1 grated carrot 3 celery stalks, chopped • 2 tbsp blanched raisins 3 tbsp chopped walnuts • 2 tbsp low-fat mayonnaise pinch of grated nutmeg • sea salt and freshly ground black pepper 6 large, deep green lettuce leaves

Combine the apple, carrot, celery, raisins, and walnuts in a mixing bowl. Add the mayonnaise and nutmeg, and mix well. Season to taste. Arrange the lettuce on two dinner plates. Place the mixed salad in the centre. Garnish with a dash of grated nutmeg. If you prefer, dress with mayonnaise or a little pineapple juice. *Serves 2*

GRILLED MUSTARD SALMON

Salmon is high in omega-3 fatty acids, which have been known to reduce arthritic inflammation. It is a good source of protein and contains vitamin A.

INGREDIENTS

2 250-g (8-oz) salmon fillets • ½ lemon • 1 tbsp chopped fresh tarragon leaves • sea salt and pepper • 1 tbsp sesame or sunflower oil • 2 tbsp Dijon mustard

Place the salmon fillets on a baking tray. Squeeze lemon juice over them. Rub with tarragon, and season. Leave to marinate for 15 minutes. Mix the oil and mustard, and coat the top, and sides of the fillets. Grill for 9–12 minutes, depending on thickness of the fillets. Serve with vegetables and lemon wedges. *Serves 2*

PITA POWER LUNCH

This is a quick, easy lunch packed with vitamins and minerals. Although avocado is high in calories, it is a gold mine for minerals; some research suggests that avocado oil lowers cholesterol. Alfalfa sprouts are unusually high in vitamin C and minerals. Like all wholegrain breads, pita bread is high in energizing B vitamins. The hot pepper boosts the metabolism.

INGREDIENTS

½ ripe avocado • 1 spring onion, chopped • sprinkle of chilli flakes or dash of cayenne pepper• 1 tbsp vinaigrette dressing 1 pita bread or other wholegrain bread • 2 soft lettuce leaves 2 tbsp fresh alfalfa sprouts • 2 slices ripe tomato

Mash the avocado with a fork to a lumpy consistency. Mix in the spring onion, chilli flakes, and dressing. Fill the pita pocket with the avocado mixture. Add the lettuce, sprouts, and tomato slices. Serve with a dressing, or add a squeeze of lemon and a dash of salt. *Serves 1*

EXOTIC MUSHROOMS & MILLET

The pungent quality of the mushrooms is balanced by the mild, somewhat neutral taste of millet. Millet is an alkaline grain, high in B vitamins, and phosphorous, which is beneficial to the nervous system. Some mushrooms, such as the shiitake variety, may contain anti-cancer enzymes.

INGREDIENTS

1 tsp olive or sesame oil • 450 ml (16 fl oz) boiling water 70 g (2½ oz) sliced mushrooms (shiitake, portobello) 1 medium-sized onion, chopped • ½ tsp sea salt 160 g (8 oz) millet

Preheat the oven to 150°C/300°F/Gas 2. Heat the oil with 2 tablespoons of water in a frying pan. Add the mushrooms, onion, and the salt and cover. Sauté until all the water has evaporated and the mushrooms and onion are tender. Pour the millet into a baking dish. Cover with boiling water. Add the mushrooms and onion and stir. Bake in the oven for 30 minutes. Take the baking dish out of the oven and allow to stand for 5 minutes. *Serves 2*

PRIMAVERA TRICOLORE

Italians know the health benefits of food that looks and smells as good as it tastes. They also know that for thousands of years, olive oil has benefited prince and pauper with its golden richness. Likewise, garlic has been used for healing and as a flavour since Roman times. This longevity-promoting Italian recipe combines a whole spectrum of vitamins and minerals.

INGREDIENTS

500 g (1 lb) spinach & tomato fettucine pastas • ½ tsp sea salt 4 tbsp extra virgin olive oil • 50 g (2 oz) broccoli florets 3 cloves garlic, sliced • 2 tbsp chopped fresh parsley • 2 tbsp chopped fresh basil • 1 small courgette, quartered and sliced • 2 tbsp sliced sun-dried tomatoes 25 g (1 oz) grated Parmesan cheese

Bring a large saucepan of salted water to the boil. Add the pasta. Cook according to the instructions on the packet or until al dente. While the pasta is cooking, heat 2 tablespoons of oil in a large frying pan. Sauté the broccoli over a medium heat for 2 minutes, then add the garlic, herbs, courgette, and the sun-dried tomatoes. Cover and cook over a low heat, stirring occasionally for another 2 minutes, until the vegetables are just tender. (Do not brown the garlic; it can become bitter.) Drain the pasta. Return it to the saucepan, adding the vegetables and the remaining olive oil. Gently mix. Serve immediately, topped with Parmesan cheese. *Serves 4*

DELHI DINNER

This is a spicy, satisfying one-dish meal that serves several people. The vegetables are very tasty and high in nutrition but moderate in calories. Tofu and yogurt contain significant calcium and protein. The grains are high in the B-group vitamins.

INGREDIENTS

4 tbsp sesame oil • 2 tbsp ghee • ½ tsp black mustard seed 2 tsp curry powder • 1 tsp ground cumin • 1 tsp ground coriander • 1 tsp ground ginger • 1 tsp chilli powder 2 tsp sea salt • ¼ tsp ground cloves • 2 medium onions, sliced 2 cloves garlic, finely chopped • 100 g (4 oz) raisins • 100 g (4 oz) raw cashew halves • 100 g (4 oz) broccoli florets 2 carrots cut into julienne strips • 100 g (4 oz) cauliflower florets • 1 small yellow squash, cubed • 100 g (4 oz) peas 200 g (7 oz) tofu, diced • 250 ml (9 fl oz) plain yogurt

Heat the oil and ghee in a heavy saucepan. Stir in the spices. Simmer over a low heat for 2 minutes or until blended. Add the onion, and sauté until softened (about 5 minutes). Add the garlic and stir. Cook for 1 minute more. Mix in raisins and cashews, and sauté for 2 minutes. Stir occasionally. Add the broccoli, carrots, cauliflower, and 50 ml (2 fl oz) of water. Cover and cook until the vegetables are almost tender (about 5 minutes). Add the yellow squash, peas, and tofu. Cover and cook until the squash is tender. Stir occasionally. Remove from the heat. Let the mixture cool for 2 minutes. Add the yogurt and stir. Serve with long-grain brown rice. *Serves 4*

PRAWN & SCALLOP ORIENTALE

This dish contains important vitamins and minerals. Prawn and scallops are rich in iodine and sodium, the carrots and broccoli are high in vitamin A, and the garlic and onion purify the blood. In addition, broccoli and cauliflower contain elements that can help to combat cancer.

INGREDIENTS

1 tbsp vegetable oil • 12 large, uncooked prawns • 12 bay or sea scallops, halved if large • 100 g (4 oz) sugar snap peas 1 carrot cut into julienne strips • 100 g (4 oz) broccoli florets 100 g (4 oz) cauliflower florets • 1 spring onion, sliced 1 clove garlic, sliced • 100 g (4 oz) sliced water chestnuts 1 tsp miso paste or 1 tbsp soya sauce • 1 tbsp sesame oil

Heat the vegetable oil in either a large heavy frying pan or a wok until sizzling hot. Add the prawns and scallops and sauté, stirring often, for 3 minutes. Remove from the pan and keep warm. Place all the vegetables, except the garlic and water chestnuts, into the hot oil. Stir-fry for 2–3 minutes. Add the garlic and stir-fry for another 2 minutes. When the vegetables are almost tender, add the water chestnuts, miso paste (mixed with a little boiling water) or soya sauce, prawns, scallops, and sesame oil. Stir and heat through for 1 minute. Serve over long-grain rice. *Serves 2*

WILD RICE STUFFING

Serve this nutritious low-calorie fare as a side dish or stuffing.

INGREDIENTS

100 g (4 oz) basmati rice • 100 g (4 oz) wild rice 1 onion, chopped • ½ tsp ground coriander • ¼ tsp ground mace ¼ tsp sea salt • 1 tsp ghee • 1 tsp sesame oil 2 tbsp sultanas • 2 tbsp pine nuts

Steam the basmati rice for 30 minutes in a covered saucepan. Simmer the wild rice for 20 minutes in an uncovered saucepan. Sauté the onion with spices and salt in ghee and oil. Add the sultanas and pine nuts when the onion is half cooked. Sauté until the onion is golden but not brown. Drain the wild rice when cooked, and add to the onion mixture. Add the basmati rice. Serve with steamed vegetables. *Serves 2*

DESSERTS

Most of us have more than one sweet tooth and all of them crave desserts! Indulge in these healthy sweets and your progress toward well-being will not be impeded.

MOM'S MOUSSE

This is a dessert I dreamed up for my children when I was trying to avoid white sugar and all those sweet disasters that children love. It actually appeals to all ages. The vitamins A and C, the minerals in the fruit, and the digestive benefits of yogurt and honey are nutritional bonuses, and this mousse is simple and quick to make.

INGREDIENTS

225 g (8 oz) mixed dried fruit • 250 ml (9 fl oz) plain yogurt • 1 tbsp honey • pinch of ground nutmeg

Cover the fruit with water, and stew in a covered saucepan on low heat for 20 minutes. Allow to stand, covered, for another 10 minutes. Blend the fruit and water for 30 seconds in a processor or blender. Add the yogurt, honey, and nutmeg to the mixture. Blend again until smooth. Fill dessert bowls with the mousse and chill. Top with a sprinkle of nutmeg. *Serves 4*

FRESH FRUIT SALAD WITH BLOSSOM HONEY SYRUP

Fragrant blossom honey is essential to achieve the delicate flavour of this dessert. The fruits are loaded with vitamin C and minerals.

INGREDIENTS

60 ml (2 fl oz) water • 3 tbsp blossom honey zest from 1 orange • 450 g (1 lb) fresh fruit (pineapple, berries, kiwis, nectarines)

Gently heat the water, honey, and zest together. Do not allow to boil. Cool. Chop or slice the fruit. Mix with the syrup. Serve in individual bowls with honey-sweetened yogurt or whipped cream. *Serves 4*

MAPLE APPLE

Apples are high in vitamin A, and contain malic acid, which is good for digestion; they make this dessert nutritious as well as delicious.

INGREDIENTS

4 large baking apples • 100 ml (4 fl oz) maple syrup (or honey) • 1 tbsp cinnamon powder • 1 tbsp rum 3–4 cloves • 1 tbsp butter • 2 tbsp chopped walnuts or pecans, lightly toasted

Preheat the oven to 180°C/350°F/Gas 4. Core the apples, but not all the way to the bottom, so the filling will be contained. Mix the maple syrup, cinnamon, and rum. (The alcohol will burn off and leave a pleasant rum flavor, but you can leave the rum out without diminishing the taste too much.) Place the apples, upright, in a shallow baking dish. Pour 2.5 cm (1 in) of water into the dish. Fill the apples with the maple syrup and rum mixture. Scatter the cloves in the syrup. Divide the butter into four, and place a portion in each filled apple. Bake the apples in the oven for 30 minutes. Top each apple with chopped nuts and eat warm or cold. This is delicious served with whipped cream or vanilla ice cream. (Take care not to eat the cloves.) *Serves 4*

RESCUE ROUTINES

*Challenges to our well-being continue to multiply as we
have less time to deal with them. In the Rescue Routines,
I have tried to throw you simple, fun lifesavers that
will not only keep you afloat but make your life far more
enjoyable. Each Rescue addresses specific problems for a day.
However, most can be beneficially pursued for much
longer. The most efficient way to use a Rescue is to plan
ahead. The night before, briefly work out how you will fit the
routine into your life. If there are others in your household,
tell them what you decide. Write the Nudge Notes suggested
for each day and place them in strategic places, such as
on the bathroom mirror. Get ready and go for it!*

ANTI~STRESS DAY

When you sense that your stress level is high, indulge in an anti~stress day with pleasurable pastimes that help break harmful habits.

CONSTANT MENTAL and physical stress, whatever the source (family difficulties, work pressure, money worries), will eventually affect your health. The immediate reaction to stress is known as the "fight or flight" response, in which the body releases several hormones to prepare it for rapid action. Although some stress is beneficial, making us stronger and more resilient, a constant flow of these hormones will, over time, damage our immune and nervous systems. Chronic stress can diminish a person's sense of wholeness and ability to love and be loved. This can happen to women, men, teenagers, and children.

My anti-stress day is designed to help you break your stress pattern and to initiate pleasurable, soul-expanding habits that you can turn to whenever you become stressed.

Ideally, choose a day when you are not working, although you can incorporate my ideas into a work day. Approach the day with a sense that you are a human being, not a human "doing". Once you have planned your day, let it happen to you. One of the reasons that people become stressed is that they feel overloaded with responsibility. Today should be a day without obligations. If there is an easy way to cook your meals, do so. If you are always helping others, ask them to help you instead. Point out that if you are more relaxed, you will be a better friend, colleague, or parent.

Focus wholly on the moment with all your senses in play. After all, yesterday is gone, and tomorrow may be completely different to what you expect. Whatever you fish for, let bliss be the catch of the day.

CALMING LAVENDER
Soak away stress in a bath scented with lavender, and dry with luxurious towels in soothing pastel colours.

PREPARATION

Today, your only objective is to feel relaxed. Buy essential oils of lavender and vetiver or sandalwood, and some chamomile or vervain tea. Choose a piece of calming music to accompany your activities.

COLOURS FOR THE DAY

Calming pastels and neutrals

NUDGE NOTES

"Bliss is the catch of the day"

"Forget yesterday and tomorrow"

"All is calm"

"Relax!"

MENU SUGGESTIONS

BREAKFAST
Fruit, yogurt and honey, wholegrain muffin. Chamomile or vervain tea.

LUNCH
Grilled chicken with salad, or large green salad with hard-boiled eggs and 60 g (2 oz) of hard cheese.

AFTERNOON
Carrot and celery juice (see p.54).

DINNER
Steamed vegetables with baked potato. Fresh Fruit Salad (see p.59).

MORNING ACTIVITIES

1 CALM START

Wake up to the sound of rhythmic soothing music rather than to an alarm. Dress in comfortable clothes made from soft, pastel-coloured fabrics. Begin your day by meditating for 20 minutes. This practice releases stress as few other self-development techniques can. As you pass through all the sensory avenues of the meditation, release all your thoughts, good and bad. Don't think, just be.

"All is calm"

2 RELAXION

Perform the 30-minute Relaxion routine calmly. If you are tense, fill the air with the scent of sandalwood or lavender, and play music that floats. Pretend that you are an aquatic creature moving effortlessly under water from one movement to another. At the end of the routine, take a few minutes to completely unwind by lying flat on the floor with a small pillow under your head. Breathe deeply for five minutes, inviting yourself to "let go" on each exhalation.

3 NATURE WALK

Walk for 30 minutes in a quiet environment, ideally in the country or in a park. Stroll along a leafy street if there are no nearby parks. If there are trees, choose one that beckons you. Put your back against the trunk, hug it with your arms, and look upwards to its very top. Experience its balancing serenity. You will feel energized and calmed. The harmony found in nature helps to bring harmony into your own life.

TREE HUGGING
Align your spinal nerves along the tree trunk – feel its calming and balancing connection.

AFTERNOON ACTIVITIES

1 LIGHT LUNCH

What you eat can affect your moods. Complex carbohydrates such as wholegrains, slow-burning sugars, and B vitamins have a calming effect. Stay away from simple sugars like cake and sweets, and avoid hot spices. Eat protein at lunch and carbohydrates at dinner (protein takes longer to digest, and carbohydrates help you sleep). A green salad with grilled chicken or eggs and cheese is ideal for lunch. Add fennel to your salad for its calming properties. Drink herbal tea, water, or fruit juice.

SALAD LEAVES

2 CALMLY BUSY

Write yourself a plan for the rest of the day, giving yourself extra time to do everything. Engage in activities that you enjoy but which are not too stimulating. Try to completely absorb yourself in whatever you do. Do not demand expertise of yourself. Just enjoy the process of your activity, and play into it with no sense of competition. Gardening, painting, or reading are all excellent stress-relieving activities. Use your spare time to catch up on letter writing, or visit an art gallery or museum. Avoid watching overly stimulating television.

3 SENSORY SHOPPING

Give yourself time to lose yourself in choosing and preparing food. Handling food can be a grounding experience since it is another connection to nature. Try to shop where food is creatively displayed and you can be unhurried in your selection. Enjoy the process of using all your senses as you choose fresh produce.

4 TAKE A BREAK

Relax for 15 minutes on the slant board (see p.9). Lie down and close your eyes. Take a few deep breaths and then breathe normally. Relax your toes, and then move up to your knees, calves, thighs, pelvis, stomach, chest, shoulders, arms, hands, neck, and face. Feel each part of your body grow heavy and sink into the board.

SLANT BOARD
Lying on the slant board reverses the normal pull of gravity, resting your internal organs and spine.

EVENING ACTIVITIES

1 DINNER

Adorn your table with flowers and fine tableware. Eat a leisurely meal, chewing well. Light food sparingly seasoned with calming herbs such as basil or marjoram will continue the soothing theme of the day. Try steamed vegetables accompanied by a baked potato with a little herb butter. Let your food settle in your stomach before starting another activity.

"Forget yesterday and tomorrow"

2 THINK QUIET THOUGHTS

After dinner, spend 10 to 15 minutes in contemplation. Choose a non-controversial subject that won't disturb your evening peace. You might select a beautiful object such as a painting or sculpture that decorates your home. Imagine how it was conceived, and think right through the creative process to the finished piece. Contemplating beauty feeds the soul as well as the eye.

3 BATHING

Luxuriating in a very warm bath with lavender- or chamomile-scented water is extremely relaxing. Light some candles, play soothing music, close your eyes, and bliss out. Dry yourself with a thick soft warmed towel.

4 RELEASE MASSAGE

Arrange a partner massage. Tight necks and shoulders are a common result of work-related stress. Massage relieves this tension. Sit on a stool and relax with your head slightly forwards and your hands in your lap. Ask your partner to massage all over your upper back, shoulders, and into the neck *(see pp.36–37)*. Use a relieving massage oil, such as lavender mixed with vetiver. Start with finger pressures underneath the skull, one hand holding the head, the other applying the pressure. Then knead the neck, shoulders, and upper back.

"Relax!"

SHOULDER MASSAGE
Use essences of lavender with vetiver in a light vegetable oil. Place the bottle of oil in hot water for a few minutes for extra strength.

SPRING~CLEAN DAY

If you feel over-fed and under-exercised, my gentle detoxifying day will cleanse your system, leaving you brighter, lighter, and healthier.

MOST OF US understand that we need to take responsibility for our own well-being. This is borne out by the ever-increasing interest in natural methods of healing. To build a healthy life you need to start with a clean foundation. New paint doesn't do very well on a flaky surface. My one-day programme will cleanse you without causing discomfort. Think of this day as a gift to your mind, body, and spirit. You are treating yourself to a chance to function at top form by eliminating the toxins that impede efficient digestion, circulation, clear thought, and inspiration.

My gentle detoxification programme can be used as a one-day refresher or pursued for several days. I do not suggest a strict fast, which would have to be supervised by a health professional. It is much better (and safer) to cut down on the quantity and increase the nutritional value of your food. You can obtain the best results from my spring-clean day if you plan ahead and enter the programme with a positive attitude about results. Choose activities and food that you enjoy. I don't care how good spinach is for you; if you hate every swallow, it won't do you much good. With so many delicious detoxifying juices and foods, fun exercises, pleasurable baths and rubdowns, you should be able to find some to enjoy. Pursue them with the knowledge that they are benefiting your entire system, and they will.

Remember that mental and emotional toxicity is just as deadly as any physical poison. Resentment, anger, frustration, and whatever put them in your life need to be dealt with and eliminated.

FRESH WATER
Drinking pure water is one of the best ways to cleanse your body. It helps to clear waste from undigested food and dead cells through the lymphatic system, which is our most important detoxification mechanism.

PREPARATION

Stock up on fresh fruit, vegetables, and spring water, and have a juice extractor ready for making fresh fruit or vegetable juice. Buy essential oils of juniper and lemon ready for a detoxifying massage and bath, and a brush for dry-brush massage.

COLOURS FOR THE DAY

Fresh spring hues

NUDGE NOTES

"Clean inside, gorgeous outside"

"Toxicity is out of my life"

"Raw is better"

"Breathe!"

MENU SUGGESTIONS

BREAKFAST
Juicy fruit with fat-free yogurt. Chamomile tea with lemon.

LUNCH
Rejuvenation Salad (see p.56).

AFTERNOON
Mineral cocktail (see p.54).

DINNER
Exotic Mushrooms and Millet (see p.57) with steamed vegetables (carrots, courgette, marrow, broccoli), or a plate of juicy fruits (pineapple, nectarine, mango) with low-fat cottage cheese topped with fat-free yogurt, dressed with a spoonful of honey.

MORNING ACTIVITIES

1 WAKE UP

Soon after rising, drink 300 ml (10 fl oz) of hot water (ideally pure spring water). Every hour thereafter, drink 120 ml (4 fl oz) of hot water. The water clears away the debris from undigested food through your lymph system. Wash with very warm water.

HOT WATER WITH LEMON

2 "DETOX" BREATHING

When you breathe, you take life-giving, detoxifying oxygen into your lungs and exhale carbon dioxide and other noxious gases. Remember that exhaling properly is as important as inhaling. Begin the 20-minute meditation with a visualization of breathing in clean air and breathing out toxins. Before exercising, stand still and breathe deeply for five minutes, placing your hands over your rib cage and feeling it expand as you inhale.

"Breathe!"

3 CLEANSING IN AND OUT

After exercising, dry-brush your skin and shower. Dry-brush from feet to head, moving in circles (see p.46–47). Shower in warm water. Enjoy the feeling of being super clean. After cleansing, eat a healthy breakfast of fresh juicy fruits and fat-free yogurt. Chamomile tea with lemon is detoxifying. If you don't like the taste, try another herbal tea or cereal coffee. Remember to drink hot water regularly throughout the day.

BREAKFAST
Juicy fruits and alkaline grains such as millet are cleansing foods since they eliminate toxins.

AFTERNOON ACTIVITIES

1 SPRING-CLEAN WALK

This should be no ordinary sauntering walk. To wake up your system you need to push your pace for about 30 minutes. Start out with an easy stride to warm up, and then walk as fast as you can with your arms bent and at waist level. Spring forwards into the freshest, most nature-rich atmosphere you can. Move from the hips to stimulate intestinal movement. Try my breathing exercise to clear your lungs. Take a six-second deep breath through the nose and a ten-second exhalation through the mouth. Repeat this exercise five times as you walk.

"Toxicity is out of my life"

2 EAT YOUR ENZYMES

Feast on a healthy lunch of raw fruits and vegetables, which contain living enzymes that scavenge the body's toxins. Eat my Rejuvenation Salad *(see p.56)* to let the enzymes work for you. If you like, add a slice of wholegrain bread without butter. Drink water with lemon, or a herbal tea such as rosehip. When you shop for your health food, choose organic produce that looks and smells fresh and wholesome. Clean the produce well before eating, and eat it while it is still fresh.

RAW VEGETABLES & FRUIT

3 MINERAL COCKTAIL

Although hot water is the main drink of the day, treat yourself to a cup of freshly extracted vegetable or fruit juice in the early evening. Vegetable juice made from liquified, fresh organic celery, carrots, parsley, and spinach is both detoxifying and delicious *(see p.54)*. An alternative to vegetable juice is freshly squeezed fruit juice. This is more nutritious than shop-bought juice. Drink the juice as soon as it is ready.

VEGETABLE COCKTAIL
If you are eating lightly, fresh vegetable juice makes an excellent food supplement. Think of it as your 5 pm "cocktail".

4 CLEARING VISUALIZATION

To clear your mind and body of toxic blockages you need to relax and let them go. My 10-minute visualization will renew all of you. Sit comfortably in a straight-backed chair with your hands turned upwards on your lap. Precede each visualization with a deep inhalation, and feel toxins leave each area of your body on the exhalation. Close your eyes and breathe into your brain, letting toxic thoughts out through your nose. Repeat this process working down the body, and visualize your blood and lymph flowing freely, clearing away any toxic obstruction.

EVENING ACTIVITIES

1 DETOXIFYING RUBDOWN

In the evening, immerse yourself in a deep, hot bath to which you have added two handfuls of pure sea salt. The salt will draw toxins out of your body. Soak for 10 minutes, dry, and then massage your entire body, using purifying essential oils such as lemon and juniper.

SELF-MASSAGE
Encourage your cells to give up their toxins by stimulating your circulation and cleansing congested tissue. Massage with upward strokes to direct the lymph into the nodes, which act as a filter.

FACIAL STEAMING
To deep-cleanse your skin, lean over a bowl of hot water scented with juniper. The steam detoxifies and hydrates your pores.

2 FAST OR EAT

An evening fast will make your spring-clean day more effective. After 5 pm, drink only hot water or a mild herbal tea such as chamomile. A less spartan approach would be to eat steamed vegetables and millet seasoned with purifying basil (use the fresh herb). Don't cook with fats or oils since they clog elimination pathways and slow detoxification. Chew well, and savour every bite.

BASIL

3 BEDTIME

Plan to go to bed early. Sleeping for eight hours will actually help your body to cleanse itself. Before drifting off, meditate for 20 minutes. As you lie in bed, breathe deeply for several minutes and visualize your entire being as cleansed and clear.

THINK~SLIM, BE~SLIM DAY

*My unique plan for light living relieves feelings of heaviness,
and reduces weight without making you feel deprived.*

DID YOU WAKE up this morning feeling fat and bloated? Try not to despair — we have the slim solution! The following programme provides activities that will take off a little weight and make you feel much better about yourself, even if pursued for only 24 hours. The important difference in my plan from the many weight-reduction programmes available is that you make yourself feel, as well as look, slimmer and fitter using all the tools already outlined in this book. From the moment you wake up, notice how you stand, move, and think about your physical appearance. If you visualize yourself as taller and thinner, you will be amazed by how much better you feel and look. In particular, use the Nudge Notes to help you visualize the happier, slimmer you.

When you make the decision to lose weight, remember that your body needs fat, tissue, and muscle to perform the necessary life-sustaining functions. Women by design carry more body fat than men. This is because they are made to bear children. Being slim does not mean being underweight but comfortable with the way your body moves and wears clothes. Excess weight stresses the body since the heart must work harder to feed blood to every bit of tissue. Being fat is also tough psychologically. Society is rarely kind to obesity. From nursery school on, overweight children can suffer unkindness from their peer group.

Find out what a healthy weight is for your height and build, and aim for that. By following this pleasurable plan for one or more days, you should be rewarded with a better shape and self-image, and more energy.

JUICY FRUITS
*Eat citrus fruits for breakfast
and as a snack for sunshine
vitamins and a natural,
low-calorie energy boost.*

MORNING ACTIVITIES

PREPARATION

Think of this day as a caring treat, not as a sacrifice. Choose one or two from the following essences: lavender, geranium, orange, and lemon.

COLOURS FOR THE DAY

Light, bright, fresh colours

NUDGE NOTES

"Move it and lose it"

"I am slimmer and healthier"

"One minute in the mouth, one month on the hips"

"Slim is in"

MENU SUGGESTIONS

BREAKFAST
Baked apple with plain oatmeal cooked with raisins.
Fruit tea.

LUNCH
Vegetable soup (see p.56) with a slice of wholegrain bread.

LATE AFTERNOON
Carrot and celery juice (see p.54).

DINNER
Steamed vegetables with brown rice or Prawn and Scallop Orientale (see p.58).
Pears baked in apple cider.

1 WAKE-UP

Dry-brush your skin and take a shower. Dress in loose comfortable clothes (this will help you to feel slim). Sip a cup of hot water, preferably chlorine-free spring water. Add a bit of lemon juice, a natural antiseptic. Since losing weight frees debris into the system that must be flushed out, drink hot water every two hours.

ANTISEPTIC LEMON

2 MEDITATION

Before you begin, and at the end of the 20-minute Mandala meditation, visualize yourself at a healthy weight. The quiet achieved through meditation allows you to focus powerfully on the image of a truly slim and fit you supported by your inner knowing.

3 GET PHYSICAL

When your mind is calm and focused on the task of the day, it is time to get physical. Perform the 30-minute Relaxion routine as energetically as possible. Jog or jump up and down in place for a few minutes at the end of the routine. Chant a mantra such as "I am slim" out loud. Motivation is key to weight loss success, and the lift that energetic exercise gives you makes you want to do more. Start early to avoid the distractions of the day.

"Move it and lose it"

JOGGING ON THE SPOT
After Relaxion, jog in place for a few minutes. This builds up a sweat and sheds water weight. Avoid a hard surface; you may injure your joints.

AFTERNOON ACTIVITIES

CYCLING
*Burn calories and
spare your joints
from impact injury
by exercising on
a bicycle.*

I LIGHT LUNCH, LIGHT YOU

Light eating makes you feel, as well as ultimately look, light. Two dietary sins to avoid are too much food and too much fat. You should always eat only to the point of satisfaction, and never beyond comfort. If food is poorly assimilated, it turns more readily into toxic tissue such as cellulite. Fats, oils, butter, and meat fat actually turn to fat. Enjoy vegetable soup *(see p.56)* for lunch, and finish with a cup of parsley tea. Simmer a few sprigs of fresh parsley in 300 ml (10 fl oz) of mineral water for approximately five minutes.

"One minute in the mouth, one month on the hips"

2 BURN CALORIES

Exercise for at least 20 minutes. Energetic exercise (known as aerobic), sustained for 20 minutes, increases your heartbeat. One hour of aerobic exertion will use up about 200 calories – the price of a wholegrain muffin.

EVENING ACTIVITIES

1 SLIMMING SAUTE

The wrong preparation can turn even the most slimming food into a fattening feast. Steaming or low-fat sauté are happy cooking solutions that preserve vital nutrients. To prepare your evening meal, pour just enough water into a shallow frying pan to cover its base. Add a teaspoon of olive oil when the water starts to boil. Add chopped vegetables, a little sea salt, and a pinch of herbs. Cover and simmer until the water evaporates and the oil flavours the food.

FRESH VEGETABLES

2 WALK MORE, EAT LESS

In the evening, take a gentle walk after dinner for about 20 minutes, visualizing the slimmer you with every step. Walking in the fresh air will speed up your metabolism and reduce your appetite, thus helping you to lose weight. Exercise with deep breathing actually produces appetite-suppressing hormones in the brain. Always try to take the scenic route since being out in nature, away from the kitchen, is usually a good antidote to food cravings. Remember to breathe deeply.

"Slim is in"

3 SEE YOURSELF SLIMMER

Visualization can be a powerful weight-reduction tool. Use it to chisel away extra weight in your mind's eye, and your cells will respond. Sit down and close your eyes. See a slimmer you performing everyday tasks. Feel your waist becoming smaller and your torso lengthening. Hold this image for ten minutes. Bring this image to mind several times a day and hold for five minutes or so.

"I am slimmer and healthier"

4 SATISFYING BATH

Before going to bed, bathe in water scented with luxurious essential oils. Uplift your spirits and satisfy your sense of smell (closely related to your sense of taste) with essence of lavender, orange, lemon, or geranium. Then treat yourself to a massage to relax your nerves and any congested, fat-holding tissue. Meditate for 15 minutes and you will sleep soundly without craving that midnight snack.

RELAXING STROKES
Self-massage can provide a sense-soothing pleasure that treats both the skin and the psyche.

GENERATE~ENERGY DAY

*This day shows you how to be more energetic, while enabling you
to maintain a sense of calm in all your activities.*

MOST OF us wish we had more energy to accomplish the ordinary tasks of each day, not to mention the extra charge needed for special challenges. Unfortunately, we often resort to artificial stimulants, such as caffeine, sugar, and nicotine, for the lift that will pick us up and fire our engines. Coffee, for example, contains 60 chemicals, including carbolic acid, which produce a quick high and an equally rapid letdown, leaving you with even less energy than before. Eventually this plays havoc with your pancreas, which controls blood sugar levels.

My energy-generation day will help you develop long-lasting, life-enhancing energy by tapping into your own inner resources with exercise, dynamic rest, and nutrition.

Energy is the key to well-being. All that you do and feel is more efficient and fulfilling if you are not hampered by fatigue. Exercise, deep breathing, sports, and brisk walking in fresh air all contribute to energy production. It's similar to investing money: you have to put energy in to be able to take energy out. The more sedentary you are, the more sedentary you will be. There should be a balance between activity and rest. Exercise, play, walk, and run up to the point of exhaustion, but not beyond. Listen to your body. If you feel exhausted, rest! The best rest, besides actually sleeping in bed for an hour, is lying on a slant board, your head 35 cm (14 in) lower than your feet. This quickly nourishes your brain cells and internal organs.

ENERGIZING FOOD
*Fresh organic fruits and vegetables
fuel natural energy and clear the
system for maximum performance.*

PREPARATION

Gather any sports equipment, such as a skipping rope. Stock up on essential oils of juniper and lemon. Sleep for at least seven hours the night before.

COLOURS FOR THE DAY

Energizing hues

NUDGE NOTES

"Get up and go"

"I have natural energy"

"Slant rest is best"

"Power eat"

"I am strong, free, and in command"

MENU SUGGESTIONS

BREAKFAST
Morning Millet (see p.55), or yogurt with wheatgerm, honey, and stewed dried apricots. Lemongrass herbal tea.

LUNCH
Pita Power Lunch (see p.57) Fresh apple or pear.

AFTERNOON
Carrot, beetroot, and cucumber juice. (see p.54)

DINNER
Delhi Dinner (see p.58) Mango or papaya slices.

MORNING ACTIVITIES

1 DEEP REST

Meditation puts you in a state of deep rest, which not only relaxes but revives. Today, inhale the scent of lemon or juniper as you meditate. See the energy flowing through your body from toes to head. Finally, focus on your solar plexus (see p.77), a centre of energy. Tell that centre that you are strong, free, and in command, and that you are in a state of relaxed power.

2 CAT MOVES

After meditating, roll into the Relaxion exercises. Do them fully and rhythmically, like a jungle cat about to spring, with attention but not tension. Breathe energy into every position. Then, walk outdoors, taking long smooth strides and swinging your arms for 30 minutes. Increase your tempo for the last ten minutes until you are almost running.

3 ENERGY BATHING

Start your bathing routine with a brisk dry-brush massage to stimulate blood flow. A cool shower or, at least, a shower or bath that finishes with cold water will wake you up (don't have a hot bath if your energy is low). Afterwards, slap yourself dry. Use the flat of your hands and slap from toes to hip, wrist to shoulder, and all over your chest, shoulders, and torso. As you do this, talk to your body. Tell it to wake up.

SKIN WAKE-UP
Slap dry to increase your circulation, awaken nerve cells, and make your skin look and feel more alive.

AFTERNOON ACTIVITIES

1 LIVE FOOD, LIVE YOU

Add living enzymes to your meals today with raw fruits and vegetables. Enzymes are the building blocks of every cell in the body. Cooking food kills enzymes. Remember that the more alive the food, the livelier you will be. Make sure your food is fresh. The longer it is stored, the more vitamins are lost.

"Power eat"

2 JUMP!

Jogging, tennis, skipping, or any sport that raises your heartbeat for 20 minutes just three times a week is a very safe energy-building programme. Over-exercising, however, can produce excess free radicals that can be detrimental to health. The rule is to exercise regularly but never to exhaust yourself.

SKIPPING ROPE
Raise your heartbeat and take off some weight by skipping rope. Make sure you breathe as you jump.

3 VISUALIZATION

Feeling tired is one of the first signs that we may be fighting illness or draining our energy reserves. Sensitivity to warning signs that we need more rest or have a physical problem can enhance our well-being. On your energy-generation day, cultivate inner awareness of fatigue by trying this simple exercise. Relax with your eyes closed. Breathe deeply and slowly for five minutes while concentrating on how your body feels.

Let your body speak to you as you breathe deeply and slowly. Are you tired? Do you ache? If you need a rest, take it.

"Slant rest is best"

EVENING ACTIVITIES

1 TIME OUT

A short break in the early evening can recharge your batteries. Although the ideal is to rest on the slant board, if it isn't at hand, try to find a quiet corner and shut your eyes for 15 minutes, or lie down in bed. Feel the energy suffuse your entire being. You will return refreshed and ready for the next challenge. After the rest, give yourself a massage. Your own hand is an energizing force. Stimulate the cells beneath your skin to work for your energy. Concentrate on the solar plexus. Visualize this area as filled with intense, energizing light.

SOLAR PLEXUS MASSAGE
The solar plexus is a nerve command centre for your autonomic nervous system. Use essence of juniper for an invigorating self-massage. Circle the solar plexus area just below the breastbone with the right hand, the energizing hand.

JUNIPER

2 SPICY DINING

Think of what you have for dinner in terms of who you will be for the next day and the next. I have suggested a curry for today – spicy food and hot peppers raise the metabolic rate. Food high in protein, such as fish, produces sustained energy, while carbohydrates, such as rice, pasta, and potatoes, provide quick energy.

CURRY SPICES

3 INSPIRATION

Recharge your mind with thought-provoking reading or entertainment. Heroic tales documenting a triumph over illness or climbing to the top of a mountain can inspire you to reach beyond your normal limitations. Spend ten minutes visualizing yourself accomplishing a challenging task with ease and effortless power. Think of creative ways to conquer new territory in whatever you do.

4 SLEEP WELL

Much is said about diet and exercise for energy but not enough about rest. If you want to function on all cylinders, you must have enough sleep. Most of us need seven to eight solid hours of sleep in order to function well. Meditating before bedtime will help you sleep peacefully. Another way to ensure a good night's sleep is to lie in bed, close your eyes, breathe deeply, and relax all of your body bit by bit.

"I have natural energy"

ACT~YOUNG, BE~YOUNG DAY

*Whatever your age, follow these renewal routines to brush away the cobwebs
of antiquated mind-sets and realize the joy of unlimited possibility.*

YOUNG IS MUCH more than a lack of years; it is a state of mind. Whatever your true age, you may wake up in the morning feeling tired and old. We all know people who seem old at 20 and young at 60. Young action is willing to take risks, and young emotions are trusting. In other words, a young outlook is open and adventurous.

Today is about taking advantage of every opportunity to live more in the moment, consciously benefiting your entire being.

YOUNG CREATIVITY
Express a youthful nature through creativity. Paint, garden, write, join an acting class, and discover your ageless talents.

To act young, you must think young. Every activity suggested for this day should be done without the "I'm too old for that" caveat. If you can't run for 20 minutes because your knees are cranky, it means that your knees are in bad shape — it's not because you are 60.

You can be young as long as you live, but first you must learn to live. Parts of you will never age, and your spirit is one of them. You can influence your body and mind if you are young in spirit. Your cells know if you are thinking old and will age measurably in response, since the body is ever-changing. You can halt and even reverse the process. Over the course of a year, almost every cell in your body is renewed. Talk to your skin, hair, eyes, teeth, heart, and bones and congratulate them on being ageless. You will see visible results in your own face from thinking "up". Let your spirits sag and so will your chin and bottom. Pretend that there is an invisible net pulling up your face. Smile from your toes to your scalp, and feel the lift from the inside out.

MORNING ACTIVITIES

PREPARATION

Select youth-promoting essential oils such as rosemary, rose, geranium, and sandalwood for bathing and massage. Buy a face mask, or the ingredients for one (lavender water and green clay).

———

COLOURS FOR THE DAY

Clear bright, "up" hues

———

NUDGE NOTES

"Think up"

"Let go and live"

"Belief becomes biology"

"Play!"

———

MENU SUGGESTIONS

BREAKFAST

Fruit and plain yogurt with a tablespoon of wheatgerm. Herbal tea with ginseng.

LUNCH

Salad with alfalfa sprouts, half an avocado, cheese, or hard-boiled egg. Garlic, olive oil, and lemon dressing. Wholegrain roll.

AFTERNOON

Carrot, beetroot, and cucumber juice (see p.54).

DINNER

Grilled Mustard Salmon (see p.56) with steamed broccoli, and marrow sautéed in sesame oil. Sliced pineapple.

I ANTI-AGEING MEDITATION

Wake up early and meditate for 20 minutes surrounded by the scent of rose or sandalwood. Begin by visualizing every cell becoming younger. Recognize that you are providing your mind and body with a deep rest that encourages repair. Meditation raises the level of DHEA (dehydroepiandrosterone), which is secreted by the adrenal cortex. The hormone gradually declines as we age, affecting our skin, hair, energy, and vital organs. Stress definitely reduces the adrenal output of DHEA, so anything we can do to relieve stress helps to reverse the decline of this anti-ageing hormone.

"Think up"

FEEL-GOOD
ESSENTIAL OILS

2 EXERCISE, EXFOLIATE, & EAT FOR YOUTH

Perform the Relaxion routine with vigour for 30 minutes. Finish by dancing to uplifting rock, jazz, or country-and-western music. Dance freely to dispel any ageing emotions such as anger and frustration. Afterwards dry-brush your skin to stimulate cell turnover (new cells equal younger skin). Shower and slap yourself dry. Breakfast on youth-promoting yogurt and fruits, acknowledging their cleansing nourishment.

EARLY WALK

A walk before breakfast clears out cellular debris that may have accumulated during sleep, and helps bone to absorb calcium.

AFTERNOON ACTIVITIES

1 LIFE FOOD

Eat and drink at least 75 per cent of your food raw today. Choose vitamin, mineral, and fibre-rich foods. Avocados, nuts, wheatgerm, wholegrains, and seeds are high in free-radical-fighting vitamin E and worth the calories. Yogurt is a good intestinal rejuvenator and a valuable source of calcium, which strengthens bones and helps to prevent osteoporosis. Drink carrot, beetroot, and cucumber juice to nourish the blood and skin.

2 VISUAL LIFT

As you go through this day, consciously visualize your face and chin lifting. Look into a mirror and smile. Lift all the way from your neck to your scalp. Imagine any small lines and bags miraculously fading.

SMILE!

3 JUMP FOR JOY

Walk energetically in the afternoon for 30 minutes. Jump and skip and jog a little. Repeat your own mantra for agelessness, such as "Age is a state of mind!" Face east, north, west, and south respectively. Open your arms and breathe deeply at each position. This is your homage to the world around you. Imagine that the power of these polarities is suffusing your entire being.

LEAP TO FREEDOM
As you jump, feel all the blocks in your mind, body, and spirit disappear into the air.

4 RESTORATIVE REST & RELIEF

Taking the afternoon off from business or chores to play and rest will restore you physically and refresh you psychologically. A good old-fashioned nap, in bed with the curtains drawn, was beneficial to you when you were four years old and will be now. Resting on the slant board will give you a quicker lift. Lie for a least 20 minutes, lightly covered if it is cool, and imagine your body relieved of gravity's pull.

"Belief becomes biology"

EVENING ACTIVITIES

1 FOOD & FANTASY

Since this is a day when you want to break out of old habits and give new meaning to everyday activity, think about a different way to have dinner. Be creative. For example, pretend you are in a foreign location that you have always wanted to visit. Set the scene in detail with soft lighting, attractive tableware, food, and flowers. Invite friends over to share the fantasy. Play exotic music as you eat the exotic food. Really enjoy the experience.

"Play!"

2 PERSONAL EXPRESSION

Many of us have creative urges that we suppress because we think we haven't enough time or talent. But personal expression through the arts is rejuvenating. Today begin a new and exciting journey of self-discovery. Pick up a paintbrush, lump of clay, scissors, pastels, bits of colourful paper, or fabric, and express!

YOUR OWN CREATION

3 FEEL-GOOD BATHING

End your day luxuriating in an aromatherapy bath filled with youth potions to renew your skin, relax your nerves, and revive your spirits. Rosemary helps to improve circulation, geranium diminishes surface veins, sandalwood calms, and rose helps to restore facial skin. Treat yourself to a face mask. You can make your own by mixing lavender water and green clay to make a thick paste (add one part water to three parts clay). After bathing give yourself an all-over massage.

SANDALWOOD

FACIAL MASSAGE
Depending on your skin type, use a very gentle preparation on your facial skin (see p.47). Essence of rose is especially good for dry, mature skin.

DELETE~DEPRESSION DAY

*Do you ever wake up in the morning feeling depressed for no particular reason?
If so, you may need this quick, uplifting antidote to everyday blues.*

THE YIN AND YANG of life guarantees that there will be downs as well as ups. This is probably a good thing; otherwise, the ups would not be fully appreciated. However, when you are down in the dumps, such a philosophy doesn't make you feel much better. There are times when we all need a physical and psychological boost to push us over the hump. Definitely seek professional help if you have been depressed for more than a few days. But if you are just feeling a little "blue", there is much you can do to turn your mood around and shine some sun on your dampened parade. Follow my enjoyable, natural, drug-free path to feeling good, and you will leave your blues behind.

BRIGHTEN UP
Surround yourself with the natural beauty of flowers and plants. Vibrant flowers, such as sunflowers, can brighten even the darkest day.

Physicians often prescribe drugs for mild forms of depression, but meditation, exercise, good nutrition, and other healthy helpers offered here might well do the trick. At least give my routines a shot. Prescription drugs have side-effects, and some drugs are addictive. The addiction we want to promote is to life, with all stops pulled out. Ease into the habit of making meaningful connections to the world around you. Family, friends, and colleagues can provide support as you make your body and mind healthier. Contact with nature is also very healing.

When you experience intense pleasure, natural brain opiates such as serotonin are stimulated, benefiting your psyche and nervous system. Activity that turns you on combined with regular meditation is your best prescription for the blues. Take these natural tranquilizers and live life to its fullest.

PREPARATION

Prepare for your delete-depression day as if it is a celebration. Buy flowers and a musical recording or video that you have been wanting to listen to or watch. Stock up on essences of ylang-ylang, basil, and clary sage.

COLOURS FOR THE DAY

Uplifting bright hues

NUDGE NOTES

"This is a fun day"

"Happiness is a hug"

"Good-bye, blues"

"Joy is in every step"

MENU SUGGESTIONS

BREAKFAST
Yogurt with Judith's Granola (see p.55) and a banana. Rosehip tea.

LUNCH
Primavera Tricolore (see p.57) or baked potato with steamed vegetables.

AFTERNOON
Carrot and celery juice (see p.54).

DINNER
Broiled white fish with steamed green beans, peas, and courgette, or turkey with Wild Rice Stuffing (see p.58) and vegetables. Maple Apple (see p.59).

MORNING ACTIVITIES

1 WELCOME THE DAY

Think positively as soon as you wake up. Greet the day with a mantra such as "I am joy". Climb out of bed with a spring in your step and dress in brightly coloured clothes. A sluggish, toxin-filled system will make you feel low so, on waking, drink a cup of hot water to flush out toxins. Continue to drink hot water throughout the day to banish mind and body toxins. Meditation is a powerful tool in the fight against depression. Begin your meditation by visualizing a happy situation. It could be a memory or a fantasy. Throughout the day, bring this image to mind. Gently push any negative thoughts aside during the meditation, and replace them with a positive visualization. As you end your meditation, breathe slowly, open your eyes, and stretch.

ROSEHIP TEA

2 RELAXION & WALK

Relaxion exercises are designed to relieve tension, so it is a great routine to perform when depressed. Feel your body opening and becoming more receptive and freer as you move. Don't hold onto anything, let it all go. This works especially well when you do the Surrender Stretch. Play music that has an expansive spirit, and scent the air with essence of ylang-ylang. Walk outside, whatever the weather. Sing, chant, jump, and run. Be grateful for the day.

"Good-bye, blues"

SURRENDER STRETCH
As you perform the Surrender Stretch (see p.32), release your anxiety and negativity.

AFTERNOON ACTIVITIES

1 MOOD FOOD

Eat nerve-nourishing foods such as fish, turkey, pasta, wholegrains, potatoes, and dairy products. These foods contain minerals and amino acids that stimulate the production of natural opiates (brain chemicals that calm) and soothe nerve endings. It is also important to keep your blood sugar steady by eating frequent small meals. The brain's fuel is glucose, and if the body goes without it for too long, the brain's sugar level drops, which can make you feel depressed. Be especially aware of combining a concentrated sweet, such as a sugary dessert, with caffeine. This can cause a serious sugar drop.

"This is a fun day"

2 CHEER UP

One of the best ways to cheer yourself up is to try to raise someone else's spirits. Take flowers to a sick friend or call up an elderly relative who lives alone. Their response will be rewarding, and you will receive as you give. One note of caution – if you are feeling very blue, someone else's pain may be hard for you to take.

JOY OF GIVING
Give colourful flowers or another uplifting gift to someone else who needs a lift.

3 A POSTIVE VIEW

Focusing on views that please you is a great way to send positive messages through neural pathways. This can happen by looking at something beautiful or through inner visualization. If you can't go to see scenic splendour, close your eyes and create it. Work with this inner sight for about ten minutes today.

BRIGHT ROSES

EVENING ACTIVITIES

① 1 DINING IN OR OUT

Delete-depression dining should be fun and nourishing. The blues can distort your normal appetite and cause you to overeat as you try to lift yourself with food. This is a day to consciously treat yourself well, and that should include favourite foods that are healthful, such as Maple Apple dessert (*see p.59*). Stay away from alcohol – it is a depressant.

APPLE
NUTS,
& SPICES

② 2 SHARE YOUR THOUGHTS

Someone who is willing to listen to your problems, who will keep what you say confidential, and whose opinions you respect can be an invaluable aid to recovery from the blues. This noble soul can be a member of your family, your spouse, or just a good friend. Share your feelings with this person in the privacy of your home or your friend's home, or over an intimate lunch or dinner in a restaurant. Even if the friend offers little advice, it will be helpful just to verbalize how you feel and to experience the comfort of companionship. One caveat: be careful not to overburden someone who is already depressed.

"Happiness is a hug"

③ 3 MASSAGE

Soothing and balancing essences, such as basil and clary sage, used for massage, are an excellent blues-chasing treatment. Mood-lifting hormones are released in the brain and skin during massage, and nerve centres are calmed. A professional massage can deliver maximum relaxation as you completely surrender to the practitioner's hands. However, you can give yourself a relieving treat with essences. Include an anti-depression solar plexus movement. Stroke the area between your breast bone and navel in a circular motion with your left hand.

④ 4 FANTASY BATHING

To end your day, bathe in water scented with ylang-ylang, while you listen to soothing music. Soak as long as you like in the water, imagining that you are a happy sea creature. Breathe deeply, inhaling the aromatic essence.

SCENTED SOAK
Bathe for at least ten minutes in very warm scented water.

MORE~TIME DAY

We live in a world governed by clocks. If you feel that your day never has enough hours in it, especially for those you love, you need my more-time day.

CONSIDER THAT all we have is time. When we have no more time, we are no longer in this world. So the way we think about and use our time is really the way that we live. If you think that you never have enough time, you won't, and you will always be in a hurry. You can remedy the situation by becoming conscious of how you use time and then incorporating the simple time-management ideas suggested here.

When you begin to consider time as your friend instead of your enemy, you will use it wisely and find that you live more fully. Your blood pressure will probably also go down: there are few things more stressful in life than feeling that you do not have enough time.

What can you do to organize your day? Make a list of priorities. What do you need to do for your job, yourself, and others in the next 24 hours? List necessary activities and also activities that you want to do but have assumed that you would not have time for. Is there something that could be cut out or curtailed? Why not put activity on a diet? Substitute time makers for time wasters.

Personal priorities can become totally skewed in our society. Often when I lecture, someone in the audience will ask how to find time to exercise or meditate or make vegetable juice. The question is asked by students, health professionals, career men and women, and homemakers. My answer is usually this: "Consider how much time you can save by taking care of yourself. Illness wastes time."

TIME SAVERS
Activity and space organizers, such as charts, boxes, and file folders, can save time and energy that is otherwise spent searching.

PREPARATION

The day before, go to a stationery shop and buy file folders and containers, plus other storage boxes and bags that will organize your desk, recipes, and cupboards. Write your Nudge Notes, and shop for quick and easy meals.

COLOURS FOR THE DAY

Timeless pastels

NUDGE NOTES

"Time is in my hands"

"Beat the clock"

"Less is more"

"There is time for everything"

MENU SUGGESTIONS

BREAKFAST

Judith's Granola (see p.55) with milk or soy milk and a banana. Apple tea.

LUNCH

Sandwich of crunchy peanut butter (natural, unsweetened) with lettuce on wholegrain bread. Apple.

DINNER

Small mixed salad with vinaigrette dressing. Grilled chicken or fish with quick-cooked greens, such as spinach. Mom's Mousse (see p.59).

1 START EARLY

It has been shown that night workers lose balance, becoming less efficient on the job. This is because we are governed by a biological cycle, which means we perform best if we go to bed and rise early. Children automatically do this. Reset your cycle to rise by 5 or 6 am and retire by 10 pm. See how different you feel.

RISE BEFORE SIX

2 MEDITATION

Meditation should be high on your priority list. The 20 minutes it takes to drop into this just-for-you place is precious little time considering the rewards. You have to plan for this time of shutting out the world in a very deliberate manner. You will find that meditation really helps your power of concentration. See how much time that saves!

3 PLAN YOUR DAY

After meditation, when your mind is clear, make a schedule for the day. Create a slot for stress-relieving activities such as Relaxion. Think of how friends and family can help to save you time. Resolve to be firm with yourself about what you eliminate from your life that takes up time. Clutter is a serious time waster. Vow to spend at least one hour sorting out clothes, magazines, cosmetics, and any other clutter.

Checklist

Tidy wardrobe ✓
Do the laundry ✓
Sew on spare buttons ✓
Throw out old clothes ✓
Pay bills
Do the shopping

RELAXION
Exercise should be high on your priority list of worthwhile activities. The shoulder stand stimulates your brain, increasing efficiency.

MORE MORNING ACTIVITIES

1 TIME WASTERS & SAVERS

On a notepad, list time wasters on one side of the page and time savers on the other. Below, make a plan, hour-by-hour, of how and when you are going to stop the time wasters and start the time savers.

You may be surprised at how very simple adjustments to your routine will give you time for other activities.

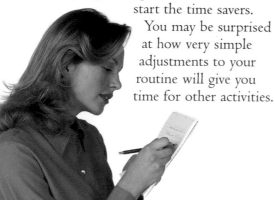

MAKE A LIST

2 ORGANIZE YOUR FAMILY

Most people long for personal time. Time to read, think, rest, or meditate. Young children, in particular, can be very demanding. The best way to give yourself a rest is to offer special books and toys that aren't your child's ordinary playtime fare. This may also help your child to understand the value of time spent alone.

CHILDREN'S PLAYTIME

AFTERNOON ACTIVITIES

3 FAST FOOD

Cooking can consume a lot of time. It is possible to cook fast food that is healthy. The trick to maximizing nutrition, while minimizing time spent cooking, is research. Learn enough about the basic vitamin, mineral, protein, and carbohydrate content of food to know how you can replace a time-consuming recipe with a quick one. A tip for fast vegetables: shred in the food processor, then sauté for two minutes in enough water to keep them from sticking to the pan.

4 SCENTED MEDITATION

Spend 20 minutes in the afternoon meditating. Scent the air with calming, psyche-expanding essences, perhaps ylang-ylang with sandalwood. These 20 minutes will be very well spent since the Mandala meditation focuses your senses and calms your mind. You will emerge refreshed, calm, and mentally alert.

ROSEMARY

5 WALK IN NATURE

Go for an unhurried walk. Observe the way nature deals with time – the seasonal life cycles come and go, in perfect balance between earth, plant, and climate. Consider that it all happens without a clock. Try to honour your natural rhythms of waking, sleeping, and hunger, free of the social dictates of "it's time to .... ".

"There is time for everything"

MORE AFTERNOON ACTIVITIES

1 TIDY AS YOU GO

To ensure that everyday items are accessible, tidy as you go. Searching through disorganized drawers, cupboards, and medicine cabinets is frustrating and time-consuming. Invest in organizers, and allot extra time today to give your clothes, makeup, personal-care items – in fact, all your clutter – a new home. Making tidying up a priority will save you time in the future. Maintain your good work by putting back whatever you take out when you finish with it.

TIDY TOOLS

2 LEISURELY DINING

Plan an unhurried evening meal. If you have children, and this means dining after they are in bed, do so. The point is to dine, not just to satisfy your hunger. Take less time in preparation and more time in consumption. Food eaten with full appreciation nourishes your spirit and body.

"Less is more"

EVENING ACTIVITIES

3 TIME FOR YOU

By the end of your more-time day, you may have some spare time on your hands. Spend this time doing exactly what you want to do – reading, watching television, or enjoying an extra-long bath. A self-massage after your bath or shower is an excellent way to reward yourself for having used your time so well.

"ME" TIME
Time spent reading literature or educational books is never time wasted: it is both relaxing and instructive.

HEALTHY-INDULGENCE DAY

*This day offers you a break from your routine with a treat or two
that won't affect your health. Pleasure can be good for you!*

HUMANS HAVE always sought ways to answer the need for joy, pleasure, and fun. To paraphrase an old saying, all work and no play makes Jack not only a dull but a very frustrated boy. However, most of us know that consistent indulgence in what is not good for us can also make us too sick and tired to have fun, even if the treat was handed to us on a silver platter. The trick is to treat yourself once in a while. Your intelligent cells know when you like what you are doing and when you don't. Even if a food, drink, or exercise is good for you, if it makes you miserable,

the benefit will be diminished. Your healthy-indulgence day, or "hi-day," should make you feel happy, not guilty. Once you decide to do it, go for it with no regrets. Self-reward definitely has its place in the well-being scheme of things.

This is a day to allow all your senses to experience pleasure. Relax and let them lead you without guilt. If you feel guilty eating dessert, taking the day off, or soaking in a bubble bath, then the benefits will disappear. What is health without enjoyment? Certainly not magical well-being. The good news is, health can be had joyfully. Once your well-being habits are in place, you won't like toxic treats nearly as much as you used to. However, the occasional treat will do you good since a physiological phenomenon takes place when you ingest food that is not your normal fare. Your adrenal glands and digestive system give a little boost to the immune system. Once a month, this is beneficial rather than harmful.

PAMPER POWER
*Occasionally making a fuss over
yourself, be it with food, beauty
products, or holidays, can provide a
real respite from routine, and can
do wonders for your well-being.*

MORNING ACTIVITIES

1 STRETCH FOR JOY

On waking, acknowledge that today you will treat yourself as a very special person. If you don't feel like following my usual routine of an early rise, meditation, and so on, then don't. However try to fit in Relaxion — it will give you a lift. As you perform the stretches, visualize joy coming through your limbs into the the centre of your being, filling your heart and mind with a warm golden light. Know that you are treating your body to life-building and life-preserving movements that nourish every organ.

UPWARD STRETCH
Take yourself out of a mental or physical slump any time during the day by reaching beyond it with a standing stretch.

2 NEW ROUTE

If you take a walk today, spark your awareness with a different route. Observe the architecture of the buildings, the grace of small animals, the variety of birdsong, and the character of the trees. Let your nose, eyes, and ears help you experience a new world outside of yourself. Take your time, and give yourself the spirit-renewing gift of discovery.

"This is my day"

3 SPECIAL BREAKFAST

Enjoy a luxury breakfast today. Lay the table using your best cutlery, napkins, and dishes. The experience should be special whether you are with a partner or alone. Remember, you are worth the treat. Make a luscious breakfast with exotic fruits, creamy yogurt with acacia honey, and crunchy wholegrain toast or a fruit or nut muffin.

MANGO

PREPARATION

Treat yourself by, perhaps, making your bed with your best linens, using fine china and silverware, and buying your favourite foods, flowers, and aromatherapy essences.

COLOURS FOR THE DAY

Warm, luscious hues

NUDGE NOTES

"I deserve a break"

"Enjoy"

"I love me"

"This is my day"

"Fun is priority no.1"

MENU SUGGESTIONS

BREAKFAST
Nutty Banana Muffins (see p.55) with tropical fruits, and yogurt. Favourite breakfast drink.

LUNCH
Grilled Chicken Salad with Curried Mayonnaise (see p.56), or aubergine, tomato, courgette, and garlic roasted in olive oil on focaccia.

AFTERNOON
Favourite tea-time treat!

DINNER
Roasted game hen, Wild Rice Stuffing (see p.58). Chicory, apple, and walnut salad. Olive oil and balsamic vinegar dressing.

AFTERNOON ACTIVITIES

1 LUNCHTIME ADVENTURE

Turn your lunchtime into a movable feast, whatever the weather. Dining differently wakes up the senses, whether by the sea or on a sun porch. Explore new possibilities and delight the taste-buds with a view that feeds all of you. If you can't take the day off work, take your lunch out to to a nearby park and nurture yourself with nature as well as food, or test out a new restaurant with your favourite friends.

"I deserve a break"

PICNIC LUNCH
Pack a basket full of your favourite foods. If you are taking the day off work, indulge in a bottle of wine with friends. Take a good rug to sit on.

2 THE PLEASURE INVESTMENT

Having yourself "done" in the most elegant spa or salon you can afford is an investment in confidence as well as an almost hedonistic pleasure. Indulge yourself in the works ... facial, massage, hair styling, manicure, and pedicure. Have a personal style analysis at a good retail store. You will emerge feeling great.

"Enjoy"

3 TEATIME FOOD TREATS

Eating something naughty once a month is positively good for you. If you are ecstatic over every bite, you are creating many happy cells and turning on your pleasure centres. Make sure that the treat is the best you can buy or make, worth every calorie, and elegantly served.

CHOCOLATE CAKE

EVENING ACTIVITIES

1 SELF-CARE EXTRAS

This is the evening for all those self-care routines that your normal day seems to deny you. A complete cleansing, toning, and nourishing of your skin should be high on your list. Use a clay mask on your face, arms, and legs. After five minutes, rinse off the mask from your face, and lightly brush off and rinse your limbs. Apply a nourishing cream to the face and lotion to the body. You will glow all over.

HOME FACIAL
Treat your skin to a face mask at home. Relax by reading or listening to music as you wait for the mask to work.

2 SLANT BOARD

Give yourself the gift of rest today. Double the benefits by lying on a padded slant board with your feet higher than your head. Lying inverted for 20 minutes is worth 40 minutes of lying flat. While your organs and circulation are relieved of their fight with gravity, your mind and body are in healing suspension. Breathe and relax. This inverted meditation renews.

"I love me"

3 SOUL FOOD

Any meal can supply "soul food" if it consists of your favourite fare and you savour every bite. Tonight's dinner should be a feast, whether enjoyed at home or at a restaurant. If you are the chef, splurge on expensive extras such as exotic mushrooms with wild rice. Set the scene with soft music and exotic flowers. Remember, you are worth it!

"Fun is priority no. 1"

4 VISUALIZATION

On this be-good-to-you day, make a special effort to tune into any discomfort in mind, body, and spirit with the intent to make it disappear. Sit quietly, close your eyes, and feel how you feel. When you have identified a problem, begin to visualize a magical healing. If the affected place is physical, visualize it as whole, healthy, and relieved of pain and toxicity. Breathe light into that part, and exhale your pain or fear. If the problem is emotional, visualize yourself fully functional, full of love and joy. Love is the wizard of psychological healing.

5 LUXURY BATHING

This is essential to a day of indulgence. Revel in a deep, warm fragrant bath that is truly a treatment as well as a treat. Let go of all mental and physical tension as the healing properties of the essences work their magic.

SENSUAL FRAGRANCE

INDEX

USEFUL INFORMATION

AROMATHERAPY
**International Federation
of Aromatherapists**
Stamford House
No. 2–4 Chiswick High Road
London W4 1TH

Judith Jackson Aromatherapy
10 Serenity Lane
Cos Cob, CT 06807
USA

Neal's Yard Apothecary
2 Neal's Yard
Covent Garden
London WC2H 9DP
Aromatherapy essential oils

**The Register of Qualified
Aromatherapists**
PO Box 6941
London N8 9HF

MASSAGE
**Association of Massage
Practitioners Training
Executive**
24 Highbury Grove
London N5 1EA

Micheline Arcier
7 William Street
Knightsbridge
London SW1X 9HL

HOLISTIC MEDICINE
**British Holistic Medical
Association**
Trust House
Royal Shrewsbury Hospital
South Shropshire SY3 8XF

**Institute for
Complementary
Medicine**
PO Box 194
London SE16 1

Natural Medicines Society
Regency House
7–107 Hagley Road
Birmingham B16 8BR

FURTHER READING
**Ageless Body,
Timeless Mind**
by Deepak Chopra, M.D.
Rider (Transworld)
Ealing, 1993.

Aromatherapy
by Judith Jackson
Dorling Kindersley
London, 1986.

**Aromatherapy,
An A–Z**
by Patricia Davis
The C.W. Daniel
Company Ltd
Essex, 1995.

**The Complete
Book of Massage**
by Clare Maxwell Hudson
Dorling Kindersley
London, 1988.

**A Natural History
of the Senses**
by Diane Ackerman
Phoenix (Little Hampton)
West Sussex, 1996.

**The Re-Enchantment
of Everyday Life**
by Thomas Moore
HarperCollins
New York, NY, 1996.

Spontaneous Healing
by Andrew Weil, M.D.
Little Brown
London, 1995.

Your Sacred Self
Making the Decision to be Free
by Dr. Wayne Dyer
HarperCollins
London, 1995.

THE INTERNET
All major internet providers
list aromatherapy, massage,
nutrition, and related services.

ACKNOWLEDGMENTS

AUTHOR'S ACKNOWLEDGMENTS

This book has been truly a co-operative venture between me and the
remarkable group of talented people that is Dorling Kindersley. From
the chairmen to the copy editors, all have understood and supported
my ideas. Especially helpful, dedicated, and patient have been my editor,
Mary-Clare Jerram and her lieutenants, Susie Behar and Debbie Myatt.
Amanda Lunn fine-tuned the graphics with great care and Jeanette Mall
has been my invaluable guide and anchor in New York. You are all magical.

DORLING KINDERSLEY

would like to thank Emily Hedges
for picture research; Irene Lyford,
Lesley Malkin, and Sally Paxton
for helpful editorial advice; Carol
Tennant for testing the recipes;
Lisa Cussans for proofreading;
and Helen Robson for design
assistance. Dorling Kindersley
would also like to thank Debbie
Flett (Crawfords) and James Highton (Gavins) for
modelling; Ian Macintosh (The Works) and Andrea Reynolds for make-
up and hair; the Theatrical Hosiery Company, London, and Simpsons of
Piccadilly, London, for exercise wear and casual clothes, and Dickens and
Jones, Richmond, for props. Joanne Harris, Richard Blair-Oliphant, and
Dita Tebby deserve special thanks for their patience and good humour.

ADDITIONAL PHOTOGRAPHY BY

Max Alexander, Philip Dowell, Neil Fletcher, Philip Gatwood, Steve
Gorton, John Heseltine, Amanda Heywood, Antony Johnson, Colin
Keates, Dave King, Sandra Lousada, David Murray, Stephen Oliver, Gary
Ombler, Roger Phillips, Colin Prior, Tim Ridley, Kim Sayer, Jules Selmes,
Stephen Shott, Clive Streeter, Grant Taylor, Andreas Von Einseidel,
Matthew Ward, Alan Williams, Steven Wooster.

By permission of the British Library (ADD L2689) p.19; Tony Stone
Images p.6 top left, p.14 top right, p.14 left, p.17 background, p.24.